Best wishes
from

Brian Aldiss

To Christopher

Wishing you a very
speedy recovery.

Your efforts are required
in the "middle"

Kindest regards
Esther & Sam Leigh.

all about CRICKET

all about CRICKET

Brian Johnston

W. H. ALLEN
A Division of Howard & Wyndham Ltd.
1972

First edition, May, 1972

Filmset in Photon Times 10 on 12 pt. by
Richard Clay (The Chaucer Press) Ltd, Bungay, Suffolk
and printed in Great Britain by
Fletcher & Son Ltd, Norwich
for the Publishers
W. H. Allen & Co, Ltd
Essex Street, London, WC2R 3JG

ISBN 0 491 00672 1

Contents

Acknowledgments

It would not be possible to write a book like this without the help and kindness of a great many people and I should like to thank very sincerely all those who have helped me for their patience and understanding, especially:

Bill Frindall for his records and statistics which I could not possibly have done myself, and for so kindly checking the proofs; the Secretariat of MCC for their good-natured answers to so many questions, and particularly Donald Carr and Brian Langley of the first class cricket office and Stephen Green, the Curator, for his untiring research on my behalf; MCC and Educational Productions Ltd for permission to use, in chapter 7, six pages of illustrations from the *MCC Guide to Better Cricket*; BBC Publications for permission to use, again in chapter 7, the field placing chart and, in Appendix 3, four illustrations of umpire's signals—all taken from *Armchair Cricket*; the Cricket Council for permission to use the LBW diagrams in chapter 8; and finally David Platt for all his patience and expert advice and for completing the vital final stages of the book with his author 13,000 miles away.

Photographs in the book appear by kind permission of: Sport and General Press Agency Ltd; MCC; Central Press Photos Ltd; *The Age*, Melbourne; John Player and Sons. Their assistance, too, is gratefully acknowledged.

Brian Johnston

Preface

All about Cricket? Let *me* say it first. What a presumptuous title, and what a claim! I plead guilty but offer extenuating circumstances in my defence. I was *asked* to write this work in this well-known 'All about . . .' series. Ever since I was seven years old cricket has played a large part in my life and for over a quarter of a century it has been my main means of livelihood.

It has given me such joy and pleasure that I thought this would be a perfect opportunity to try to bring cricket into other people's lives—especially into those of the young people for whom this series is mainly intended. It is vital for the future of the game that it is 'sold' to young people in an era when there is such great competition from so many other activities. This book will be, I hope, a useful and interesting guide as to what cricket *is* all about and should also encourage its readers not only to play, watch, or just read about it, but to *live* the game. If they do they will never regret it—and that is a claim for which I *don't* apologize.

Brian Johnston

1. The Ashes

Wednesday, February 17th, 1971, was one of the most thrilling days of my cricketing life. I was commentating on the radio to Australia and Great Britain at the moment when Ray Illingworth's England Team regained the Ashes at Sydney. From what I have heard since, this exciting moment of cricket history, was heard by listeners all over the cricketing world at varying times of the day and night . . . 'Underwood to Jenner, Jenner snicks it on to his pad, Fletcher has caught it at silly point, he's caught it, England have won back the Ashes after twelve years and the England team are chairing their Captain, Illingworth, off the field . . .'

These were the words I used at the time and how proud and lucky I felt to be on the air just then. It is an emotional moment—this winning of the Ashes—especially after touring round with a team and sharing all its triumphs and disasters.

Some people think that the Ashes are to blame for a lot of the slow play and safety-first tactics we see during an England *v.* Australia series. They reason that the side holding the Ashes has only to draw the series to keep them and so is tempted to take few risks in order to win. There is certainly some truth in this and recently most Captains have said that they would be in favour of fighting each series separately and doing away with the Ashes. But I believe on balance that it is better to keep things as they are. The Ashes are part of cricket history and cricket is a game of tradition.

What exactly *are* the Ashes and how did they come about? The Ashes are to cricket what the World Cup is to football, or the Derby to horse-racing. 'They' are the supreme challenge and the most coveted of all cricket trophies and yet they can only be won by two of the cricketing countries, England or Australia. Their origin goes back to August 1882 when Australia beat England by 7 runs at the Oval and so won their first

Test victory in England. On the following day the *Sporting Times* published a mock obituary for English cricket as follows:

In affectionate remembrance
of
English Cricket
which died at the Oval 29th August 1882 deeply
lamented by a large circle of sorrowing friends and acquaintances
R.I.P.
N.B. The body will be cremated and
the Ashes taken to Australia

In the following winter (1882–83) the Hon. Ivo Bligh took a team to Australia and won two of the three Test Matches played. At the end of the third match some ladies burnt a bail and sealed the Ashes in a small urn and presented it to the England captain, later the 8th Earl of Darnley. The urn remained his private property until his death in 1927 when it was bequeathed to MCC and is now kept in the Imperial Cricket Memorial Gallery at the back of the Pavilion at Lord's. The Ashes therefore exist but, although played for, never leave Lord's.

The Ashes have been won and held as follows:

1882–83   Presented to Hon. Ivo Bligh and held for 22 days
1882–83*   Won by Australia in Australia and held for 1 year 174 days
1884   Won by England in England and held for 7 years 174 days
1891–92   Won by Australia in Australia and held for 1 year 205 days
1893   Won by England in England and held for 4 years 160 days
1897–98   Won by Australia in Australia and held for 6 years 31 days
1903–4   Won by England in Australia and held for 3 years 345 days
1907–8   Won by Australia in Australia and held for 4 years 3 days
1911–12   Won by England in Australia and held for 8 years 342 days
1920–22   Won by Australia in Australia and held for 5 years 210 days
1926   Won by England in England and held for 4 years 4 days
1930   Won by Australia in England and held for 3 years
1932–33   Won by England in Australia and held for 1 year 187 days
1934   Won by Australia in England and held for 18 years 362 days
1953   Won by England in England and held for 5 years 170 days

* After Bligh had defeated Murdoch's Australians 2–1 in the scheduled 3-match series, an extra match was played—and lost—against a stronger, combined Australian team. This has to be treated as a separate 'series' otherwise the Ashes would have never been Bligh's.

The Ashes.

1958–59   Won by Australia in Australia and held for 12 years 12 days
1970–71   Won by England in Australia and held for ??????

On their return to England in March 1971 the whole MCC team
recorded a song on Decca F13175 entitled 'The Ashes Song'. The music

is a traditional old music hall tune, the original words of which were 'Show me your Winkle Tonight'! After the Ashes had been won we put new words to this tune and here they are:

The Ashes Song

We've brought the Ashes back home
We've got them here in the urn
The Aussies had had them twelve years
So it was about our turn
But oh! what a tough fight
It's been in the dazzling sunlight
In spite of the boos of the mob on the hill
We've won by two matches to nil

When we arrived people said
The Aussies would leave us for dead
But we knew we would prove them wrong
And that's why we're singing this song
But oh! the feeling is great
For losing is something we hate
So Sydney we thank you for both of our wins
But not for those bottles and tins

Our openers gave us a good start
And the others then all played their part
We usually made a good score
Seven times three hundred or more
The Aussies however were apt
To collapse at the drop of a hat
If they were bowled any ball that was short
It was ten to one on they'd be caught

In the field it was often too hot
So sometimes we felt very low
Whether rain was forecast or not
We always knew we'd have Snow
So now to go home we are free
And we're sure the Aussies agree
Though the series has been a long uphill climb
We've all had a real bumper time.

How's That!

2. The Story of Cricket

The story of cricket is not easy to write. There is no definite beginning and so far, thank goodness, no end. Nobody knows when it started and, in spite of some critics who have forecast its demise for the last seventy years or more, it is still very much alive. One can only imagine that many hundreds of years ago some boy started throwing stones at a friend who, to protect himself, picked up a stick and tried to hit them back. The derivation of the word cricket could easily come from the shepherd's crook which would have made the best available bat and could account for the curved shape of the early bats. They were not unlike a hockey stick—a shape very suitable for dealing with the bowling of those days which was usually along the ground. Similarly the wicket, which was originally two stumps with one bail, could have started life as the small wicket gate through which sheep entered a field or pen.

As far back as 1272 there is mention of King Edward the First's son, Prince Edward, playing *Creag*, and this is surely sufficient proof that cricket was already a game by then. But the first definite proof seems to be a manuscript dated January 16th, 1598, which is now in the possession of the Mayor of Guildford. It refers to a Surrey coroner, John Derwick, 'Playing at crickett' when he was 'a scholler of the free school of Guildford'. From then on there are various references in 1622, 1647, and 1654 to people being fined for playing cricket on Sundays. It had even spread overseas as Cromwell's generals are said to have 'prohibited crickett' in Ireland. It seems likely that, with Cromwell in power in England, the game caught on with the nobility who, with no court in London, retired to their country estates. They found that cricket was not only fun to play but that it also provided them with an opportunity to gamble. Whether we like it or not much of the cricket played from then on was the occasion for betting on the results of matches.

All evidence shows that the early development of cricket centred on the counties of Hampshire, Kent, Surrey and Sussex, and also on London itself. In fact, the first surviving score sheet is of Kent *v*. England at the Artillery Grounds in the City of London on June 18th, 1746—Kent winning a four-innings match by 1 wicket, and 18 being the highest individual score. There are various accounts of other matches during this period, at Penshurst, Kensington Gardens, Mitcham, Chivedon, and above all at Hambledon, a small village just north of Portsmouth. A short account of this famous club will help more than anything else to show what cricket in the eighteenth century was like and how its laws gradually developed.

The club was formed some time around 1750 and its first Captain and Secretary was Richard Nyren, landlord of the *Bat and Ball* Inn, which was situated alongside Broad Halfpenny Down, the ground on which

Five stages in the development of the cricket bat.

they played. This small village attracted players from the surrounding districts and became strong enough to take on and beat the full strength of England. They took part in the first recorded tie—against Kent in 1783. 'Old' John Small, their best batsman and a bit of a dab at the fiddle when the game was over, made the first recorded century—136 *v.* Surrey. Richard Nyren's son, John, in his *Young Cricketer's Tutor* has brought to life many of their players—Thomas Brett, who bowled fast and straight lobs (there was no over-arm or round-arm bowling yet), and Tom Sueter who kept wicket to him with no gloves or pads, supported by George Leer 'as sure as a sandbank' at long-stop. Both Sueter and Leer had fine tenor voices and led the singing in the *Bat and Ball*. Then there

The Bat and Ball Inn, Broadhalfpenny Down, Headquarters of the Hambledon Cricket Club.

How's that!

An example of cricket dress in the second half of the nineteenth century.

was the left-handed gipsy, Noah Mann, a fine all-rounder and horseman who rode twenty miles to play. Their greatest bowler and the most accurate of his time was David Harris, and, as Hambledon's fortunes began to decline, 'Silver Billy' Beldham appeared, a prolific run-getter who came from Farnham in Surrey but played for Hambledon.

Towards the end of the century London became more and more the centre of cricket. Betting on the game was increasing and as early as 1774 it became necessary to standardize various weights and measurements, some of which are still the same today (e.g. the weight of the ball between $5\frac{1}{2}$ and $5\frac{3}{4}$ ozs, and the width of the bat $4\frac{1}{4}$ inches). There was also the first mention of an LBW law at this time. Thus the game gradually

Two stages in the development of stumps. The third stump was added in 1776 and it was not until 1785 that two bails were used.

developed and in 1775 Hambledon played Kent in a 5-a-side match at
the Artillery ground. When John Small went into bat, 14 runs were
needed. He got the runs all right but in the process several balls from
'Lumpy' Stevens passed between the two stumps. Accordingly a third
stump was added, although the size of the wicket remained the same.
About ten years later a second bail was also added and the wicket began
to look like the one we know today.

At this time the *White Conduit Club* was flourishing at Islington but
its members wanted to find another ground as new buildings were ruin-
ing their privacy. They therefore asked a Yorkshireman living in London
called Thomas Lord to find them a new ground. He agreed and chose a
piece of land in Marylebone where Dorset Square now stands. He took
out a twenty-one-year lease and the first match was played there in 1787,
and in that year the members of the White Conduit Club formed the
Marylebone Cricket Club—the MCC. A year later MCC revised the
laws as they then stood ('hit wicket' became a way of dismissal, and a
batsman could only be out lbw if the ball pitched between wicket and
wicket). From that day MCC became the unofficial rulers of the game—
responsible for its administration and laws.

When Thomas Lord's lease ran out in 1808 he negotiated for a new
piece of land at North Bank, Regent's Park. This was only used for three
seasons and then building and railway development forced Lord to move
once again. So still with his original turf from Dorset Square he moved
to the present site of Lord's in St John's Wood, where the first match was
played on June 22nd, 1814. Since then, Lord's has been the acknowledged headquarters of cricket. From then on the development of cricket
to the game we know now received a new impetus, and it spread rapidly
throughout the country. There were a lot of 'firsts' round about this time
too. The first Gentleman *v.* Players was played in 1806, the first
recorded score of 200 was 278 by William Ward for MCC *v.* Norfolk at
Lord's in 1820, and the first University match took place in 1827. Incidentally, playing for Norfolk in that 1820 match was a seventeen-year-
old batsman—Fuller Pilch, who later played for Kent and was one of the
greatest batsmen ever. By 1835 round-arm bowling was finally legalized
in a thorough revision of the laws by MCC which included standardizing
the length of the bat to its present 38 inches and the introduction of the
'follow on' rule.

At about this time also County cricket began to get on to an organized
footing and county clubs were formed—Sussex being the first in 1839.

Famous names appeared in the score sheets—John Wisden, who later

A picture of early cricket being played overseas—Melbourne Cricket Ground, 1864.

published the first *Wisden Almanack* in 1864, and who bowled ten batsmen in one innings for North *v.* South, and George Parr after whom Parr's tree at Trent Bridge was named. Alfred Mynn the 'Lion of Kent', over 6 feet tall and weighing 20 stone, and Felix, also of Kent, who was as stylish a batsman as he was an artist. With the opening of Trent Bridge by William Clark in 1838 cricket for the first time had become popular in the North, and Clark organized an All-England XI which travelled round the country playing every type of club, large and small.

Then in 1859 came a milestone when a team of English cricketers captained by George Parr set sail for Canada to become the first-ever cricket touring team. Nine years later a team of Australian Aborigines visited England. These events provide us with a good opportunity to check on how cricket had spread overseas. The starting dates are all rather vague, but it is clear that in most cases it was the British Army or Navy who introduced cricket to the colonies.

In Australia a British Colony was established at Botany Bay in 1788 and no doubt they played cricket. But it is not until 1830 that we find the first account of a game played in Sydney and the formation of the first club in Hobart, Tasmania, two years later. In 1845 the Melbourne CC was formed and with the same initials as our own MCC similarly became the centre of administration. The game soon spread to all the

The second team from England to tour Australia (1863). The team was captained by George Parr.

other states and it took such a hold that the catering firm of Spiers and Pond sponsored the first-ever teams from England to visit Australia in 1861 and 1863. Both incidentally made a good profit. In 1876 another team came from England, captained by J. Lillywhite, and in March 1877 they played the first-ever Test at Melbourne, which Australia won by 45 runs. Finally, the Australian cricket scene was complete when the Earl of Sheffield donated 150 guineas for the promotion of cricket among the States and the Sheffield Shield competition came into being. At first only New South Wales, South Australia, and Victoria competed, but Queensland joined in 1926 and Western Australia in 1947, winning the Shield at their first attempt.

Cricket in *South Africa* was undoubtedly introduced by the British Army, which occupied the Cape at the end of the eighteenth century and the Cape Colony was the first centre of cricket in South Africa. But, as in Australia, it soon spread—Natal, Orange Free State, and Transvaal all forming clubs in quick succession. The first English team under C. A. Smith toured South Africa in 1888–89, winning both their Test Matches, and, in the same season, Sir Donald Currie presented the Currie Cup for competition between the leading provinces.

Because of the amount of sea travel involved, cricket in the *West Indies* developed far more slowly. It seems to have started in Trinidad,

Barbados, Jamaica, and British Guiana (now Guyana) in the early eighteenth century. However, it was not until 1894 that a team from England visited the islands, and the first official MCC tour did not take place until 1911. Similarly, regular organized competition between the islands was difficult to arrange. It is only during the last fifteen years or so that air travel has made visits between the islands practical, resulting in the formation of the Shell Shield Tournament in 1965–66.

Cricket in *New Zealand* did not really begin until the second half of the nineteenth century, the first inter-provincial match taking place on North Island in March 1860 when Auckland played Wellington. Four years later the first first-class match was played on South Island, Otago beating Canterbury at Dunedin. A team from England under the captaincy of George Parr also played four matches in that year, while James Lillywhite's team visited New Zealand after their Australian tour of 1877. One year later the first Australian team came over on their way to England. But it is remarkable that these two near neighbours—in spite of occasional unofficial visits—have only played one official Test Match (in 1946). New Zealand's inter-provincial competition is the Plunket Shield, presented by Lord Plunket when Governor-General in 1906, the first match being played in 1907.

Although *India* came late on to the Test scene, thanks to the British Army, cricket dates back to well before the start of the nineteenth century, although first-class cricket was not played until 1892. The first English team came out under G. F. Vernon in 1889, but the first MCC Team to play Tests in India was that captained by D. R. Jardine in 1933–34. Until the start of the Ranji Trophy Competition in the same year, first-class cricket had been rarely played but since then it has flourished.

Pakistan, of course, only became a separate cricketing country after partition in 1947. But in 1952 they were playing their first Test against India, and by 1957 had already chalked up victories against both England and Australia.

The countries I have mentioned are the 'senior' members of the International Cricket Conference and as such are the only countries to play Test Matches. But cricket has been played wherever British influence has existed and that, at one time or another, has meant virtually the whole world. In Europe, Holland and Denmark are the main contenders and many club tours are arranged between them and England. Portugal, Germany, and Italy have all been cricket strongholds from time to time and, believe it or not, English—not French-cricket is played in Paris, North, Central, and South America, Canada, Fiji, Hong Kong, Egypt, Kenya, Nigeria, Burma, and Malaysia. The list is never-ending— even Turkey and Greece have been known to stage a game. Such is the appeal of cricket—loved by many and yet completely incomprehensible to many others. But whenever two or three of British stock are gathered together you can be sure that cricket will be played so long as they can 'bully' enough of the 'natives' to join them!

The return from Australia in 1864 of the second English touring team heralded one of the most important years in English cricket. Over-arm bowling was at last legalized. Surrey became the first-ever County Champions and the first issue of *Wisden's Cricketers' Almanack* was published. Even more important, two days before his sixteenth birthday, W. G. Grace made his first appearance in big cricket, scoring 170 and 56 not out for South Wales Club *v.* Gentlemen of Sussex. From then on this bearded giant of a man strode supreme across the English cricket scene until just after the turn of the century. He actually played his last game of cricket in July 1914, a few days after his sixty-sixth birthday. During that time he *was* Cricket to the whole of England. People travelled miles in their gigs or pony carts to catch a sight of him playing. For over thirty-five years he hit the headlines. He was to cricket then, what today Lester Piggott is to racing, or George Best to soccer. He created many records in first-class cricket. He was the *first* to make 2,000 runs in a season; to do the double of 1,000 runs and 100 wickets; to score 200 and 300 runs in an innings; to reach 100 centuries; to make 1,000 runs in May. It is impossible to compare fairly cricketers of one generation with another. But remembering the bad pitches on which he had to make most of his runs, there has surely never been a greater cricketer, nor a more powerful personality. Cricket built on the foundations of his success, and from the day he appeared on the scene developments came thick and fast.

In 1868 the first touring team to visit England was a team of Aborigines from Australia and in 1876–77 Lillywhite's team toured Australia and played the first-ever Test Match at Melbourne in March 1877. This was quickly followed by the first Australian team to tour England under the captaincy of D. W. Gregory, and they caused a sensation by beating MCC in a single day by 9 wickets. 1880 saw the first Test Match in England when England beat W. L. Murdoch's side by 5 wickets. Two years later Australia had their revenge at the Oval by winning by 7 runs in the famous match, which created the Ashes (see page 9).

So Test cricket was well and truly launched and MCC ensured the universal development of cricket by a complete revision of the Laws of Cricket in 1884. Except for occasional amendments they were not again fully revised until 1947. South Africa, New Zealand, England, and Australia—in that order—all set up their own Boards of Control and in 1909 the Imperial Cricket Conference was set up, with England, Australia, and South Africa the original members. The County Championship, which had started in 1864, took some time to catch on and by 1890 there were still only eight counties competing: Sussex,

W. G. Grace—the great cricketer.

Nottinghamshire, Surrey, Kent, Yorkshire, Middlesex, Lancashire, and Gloucestershire. But by 1899 all but two of the present seventeen were included: Northamptonshire joining in 1905 and Glamorgan in 1921. Two years later the Minor County Championship was reorganized on its present basis.

All this time, of course, there were many great cricketers playing first-class cricket and I am conscious of the fact that I have so far only mentioned one, W. G. Grace. But it is difficult to strike the right balance between giving a catalogue of names and the danger of mentioning too few. However, from Australia there were W. L. Murdoch, Australia's first captain over here; C. Bannerman, who scored the first-ever Test hundred (165 n.o.) in his first Test innings; F. R. Spofforth, 'the Demon' who took the first Test 'hat-trick'; G. J. Bonnor, the big hitter; G. Giffen and C. T. B. Turner, two great bowlers and J. M. Blackham, a magnificent wicket-keeper.

For England there was Arthur Shrewsbury, about whom W.G. said, 'Give me Arthur,' when asked which batsman he rated the highest; A. E. Stoddart, a 'Rugger' International and fine athlete who captained England to victory in the 1894–5 series; R. Peel, possibly the greatest of all the Yorkshire slow left-arm bowlers; A. C. Maclaren, whose 424 is still the highest individual score ever made in first-class cricket in England; K. S. Ranjitsinhji—'Ranji'—one of cricket's greatest stroke players; the Hon. F. S. Jackson—'Jacker'—who never toured overseas, but who was a super Test batsman, a good bowler, and not only won the toss five times in the 1905 series but also topped the batting and bowling averages and won the rubber; G. A. Lohmann, a match-winning, medium-pace bowler; and T. Richardson and W. H. Lockwood, a great fast-bowling partnership.

Just before the end of the century the Board of Control was set up by the counties to run Test Cricket in England and in 1899, for the first time, there was a Test series of *five* matches in England. In the same year a record was made which still stands today—the highest individual score in *any* class of cricket. This was 628 not out by A. E. J. Collins for Clark's *v.* North Town, a junior house match at Clifton College. Even if he made 0 in all his other innings he must still have had a very good batting average at the end of the season!

For the next fourteen years cricket in England reached perhaps its highest peak. I myself would call it the 'Golden Age', though some writers give this accolade to the last decade of the nineteenth century. But just look at the names of some of those who played in this period, to which should be added most of those already mentioned. For

England: C. B. Fry, G. Gunn, P. F. Warner, J. T. Tyldesley, G. H. Hirst, G. L. Jessop, W. Rhodes, J. B. Hobbs, F. E. Woolley, S. F. Barnes, R. E. Foster. For Australia: M. A. Noble, C. Hill, V. T. Trumper, W. W. Armstrong, W. Bardsley, J. Darling, S. E. Gregory, C. G. Macartney. For South Africa: G. A. Faulkner, H. W. Taylor, P. W. Sherwell, R. O. Schwarz, A. D. Nourse, Senior. These are only a few of the great players of that time during which the first MCC Team went to Australia (1903), South Africa played their first Test in England (1907), the Imperial

Sir John (Jack) Hobbs—the Master.

Cricket Conference was constituted (1909), and the first and only Triangular Tournament was played between England, Australia, and South Africa (1912).

The period between the two wars saw the entry of the West Indies (1928), New Zealand (1930), and India (1932) into Test Cricket. But inevitably the main 'enemy' was Australia, who swamped England for eight years after the war, thanks to some superb fast bowling by J. M. Gregory and E. A. McDonald, backed up by the spin of A. A. Mailey, and great batting strength made up largely from the pre-war batsmen. In reply England had to offer J. B. Hobbs and H. Sutcliffe as the most successful-ever Test opening batting partnership, and M. W. Tate and H. Larwood as top-quality medium and fast bowlers respectively. Larwood was to be at the centre of cricket's greatest storm—the body-line series between England and Australia in 1932–3—a tour which nearly brought cricket relations between the two countries to an end. But looking back over the twenty-year period, we see that three batsmen stand out above everything and everybody else (even that superb spin-bowling partnership of O'Reilly and Grimmett): J. B. Hobbs—the 'Master'—the greatest batsman ever on all types of pitches who made more hundreds (197) and more runs (61,237) than any other player to date. D. G. Bradman—the 'Don'—cricket's greatest run-making machine who in far fewer innings than Hobbs (338 compared to 1,315) scored 28,067 runs (an average of 95·14 against Hobbs' 50·65), made 117 hundreds and in fifty-two Tests averaged 99·94! And thirdly, not far behind, W. R. Hammond, a more brilliant bat than either and a fine medium-pace bowler.

Before the start of the Second World War, England had regained the Ashes in 1926, lost them in 1930, regained them in 1933, and lost them again in 1934. South Africa had won their first Test in England (1935). The West Indies, New Zealand, and India were elected members of the Imperial Cricket Conference (1926) and four-day Test Matches were played for the first time in England in 1930.

When first-class cricket restarted after the war in 1946, the same pattern emerged as in 1919. For seven years Australia were on top and then as before the position was reversed for a time with England holding the Ashes for six years, Australia for the next twelve, and England finally regaining them in 1971. All the other countries, except New Zealand, were to defeat England in this country: the West Indies in 1950, Pakistan on their first tour in 1954, and India in 1971. Cricket lovers had been starved of cricket for five years and the crowds flocked to the

Harold Larwood bowling to his famous body-line field in Brisbane, 1933.

grounds to see personalities like Hutton, Bedser, Compton, and Evans. 1947 will always be remembered as the 'Golden Year', when both Compton and Edrich made over 3,000 runs, Compton making 3,816 and scoring 18 hundreds, two records which still stand. Hobbs had been The Master batsman, Bradman the run machine, and now Compton was the entertainer.

Both Bedser and Evans, too, can claim to have been the best in their own field: Bedser being the first English bowler to take 200 wickets in Tests, and Evans the first and only wicket-keeper to have over 200 Test victims. And last but not least, L. Hutton—the first professional ever appointed to captain England regularly. He captained the team which regained the Ashes in 1953 and his batting for its pure technique on all pitches came nearest to that of Hobbs. Many other fine cricketers have played for all the Test countries since the war and it is impossible in a short history like this to mention any but the most exceptional. G. S. Sobers, for those of us who never saw W. G. Grace, the greatest all-rounder the world has ever seen; R. N. Harvey, arguably the best of Australia's left-handed batsmen; the three Ws, Worrell, Weekes, and Walcott from the West Indies; R. G. Pollock and B. A. Richards for South Africa; Hanif Mohammad of Pakistan; R. R. Lindwall and K. R. Miller of Australia. If I don't stop now I shall go on for ever. But finally two names, or else I shall never dare go back to Yorkshire. A certain F. S. Trueman took his 300th Test wicket in 1964 and his final tally of 307 is still a record. And a Yorkshire exile, J. C. Laker in 1956 took 19 for 90 against Australia—the one record which surely *must* stand for ever.

In the quarter of a century since the end of the Second World War there have probably been more changes in the organization and laws of the game, than at any time in its history. In 1947 there was a major revision of the laws, the first since 1884 and a year later the first five-day Tests were played in England. In 1963 the amateur was abolished in English First-class Cricket and in 1965 the Imperial Cricket Conference became the International Cricket Conference. But by far the most important change was the introduction of limited over cricket or 'instant' cricket as it has become known. The Gillette Cup was started in 1963 and the John Player League in 1969. Both have been tremendous successes and have brought to the grounds many thousands for whom, in this jet age, three-day cricket has become far too slow. Spectators want to see a result all in one day and the popularity of these two competitions has done much to help the financial position of the counties, many of whom have been in dire economic straits.

But this is nothing new. Cricket has always been 'broke'. In the old days it depended on the generosity of rich patrons, now it has to rely on proceeds of football pools and of sponsors. There is no doubt that sponsorship will spread even to the County Championship, Test Matches, and to a possible World Cup. The large sums put up by the sponsors are necessary not only to meet the loss of revenue due to falling gates but also to match the ever-rising costs of running a county side. Cricket is as popular as it ever was. County membership is higher than ever, more people are playing cricket, reading about it, watching or listening on TV and Radio. For over seventy years its approaching death has been regularly announced. In 1972 I am happy to announce the following bulletin:

'Cricket is very much alive'

3. The Organization of Cricket

There are many different forms of cricket played in Great Britain—Test Matches, first-class cricket, Minor Counties, Knockout, and League competitions played by first-class cricketers, League, Club, Village, Women's, University, and School cricket. They all come under the first-ever *official* governing body for cricket—The Cricket Council. Before the Council's creation in 1969, MCC—a private member's club—had, by worldwide consent and good will, been accepted as *unofficially* responsible for the legislation of cricket.

MCC was formed in 1787 by members of the White Conduit Club, for whom Thomas Lord had opened his first ground in Dorset Fields, St Marylebone. MCC stands for **Marylebone Cricket Club**. The members inherited from White Conduit the task of framing the laws. Then at the beginning of this century the counties asked MCC to set up:

1. The Advisory County Cricket Committee to run the County Championship.
2. The Board of Control to organize Test Matches in England.

MCC itself was asked to organize all overseas tours.

In 1966 the Sports Council was set up by the Government with power to grant financial aid to all sports. They therefore asked MCC to set up an *official* body to run cricket, as they would not be able to deal with a private club. This led to the formation of the Cricket Council, which is twenty-eight strong and has three executive wings. Its structure is as follows:

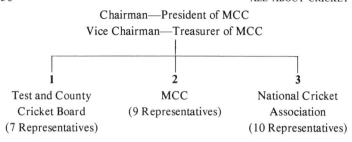

1. Test and County Cricket Board
Now does the job of the Advisory County Cricket Committee and the Board of Control. It is composed of one member from each of the first-class counties, two representatives of the Minor Counties, and three from MCC. It is responsible for:

(a) All Test Matches and first-class cricket in this country.

(b) All overseas tours, though the teams are still known as MCC.

(c) All knock-out and League Competitions played by first- or second-class cricketers.

(d) Minor Counties Cricket.

2. MCC
Provides Lord's as the headquarters of cricket and all secretarial and administrative assistance. It is still responsible for the laws of cricket and for any changes made in them after consultation and agreement with all the overseas cricketing countries. A new law can only be made, or an old one changed, by the vote of MCC members at a General Meeting of the Club.

3. National Cricket Association
Is responsible for all other grades and interests of cricket not covered by the Test and County Cricket Board. It is composed of representatives from Clubs, Schools, the Combined Services, Women's Cricket, the Universities, the Headmasters' Conference, and Umpires. It can also co-opt representatives from the National Playing Fields Association and the Central Council of Physical Recreation.

In addition there is the **International Cricket Conference** founded in 1909 by England, Australia, and South Africa, which until 1965 was

A match in progress at Lord's—home of MCC since 1814

called the Imperial Cricket Conference. *Full* membership is confined to governing bodies of cricket in countries within the British Commonwealth,* where Test Cricket is played. India, New Zealand, and the West Indies were elected in 1926, and Pakistan in 1952.

When the Conference was renamed in 1965 new rules were adopted to allow election of full or associate members from *outside* the British Commonwealth. Ceylon, Fiji, and the United States were elected Associate Members in 1965, Bermuda, Holland, Denmark, and East Africa in 1966, Malaysia in 1967, and Canada in 1968. A full member is still a country whose representative team is accepted as qualified to play Test Cricket.

The Conference normally meets at Lord's each year for two days in July to approve the various overseas tours, discuss possible changes in the laws, qualification rules for Test cricketers, and any other matters of interest. Each country sends its own representatives but to the regret of most people they have no executive power, so that few effective or important decisions are ever reached at the Conference.

* When the South African Government withdrew from the Commonwealth on May 31st, 1961, South Africa under the then constitution automatically ceased to be a member of the Imperial Cricket Conference. However, under the new rules of 1965 South Africa became eligible to be re-elected as a full member although she has not yet applied for re-election.

4. The Main Competitions

In addition to the hundreds of club, village, university, service, women's, and school matches played all over Great Britain the main competitions are:

1. The County Championship
2. The Gillette Cup
3. The John Player League
4. The Benson and Hedges Cup
5. The Minor Counties Championship
6. The Leagues in the North, Midlands, Scotland, and Wales
7. The National Club Knock-out
8. The Cricketer Cup for Old Boys' Teams
9. The Haig National Village Championship

1. The County Championship

Seventeen counties compete in the County Championship, each playing twenty matches. Illogically this means that each county meets at least once, but plays a return match against only four of the others. If two or more sides are equal on points the side with most victories is the winner.

The Awarding of Points
Points are awarded as follows: 10 points for a win, 5 points to both sides in the case of a tie, and *no points* for a first innings lead.

Bonus Points
One point is awarded to the batting side for every 25 runs scored above 150 during the first 85 overs of the first innings, i.e. 1 for 175 runs—2 for 200—6 for 300. Similarly, one point is awarded to the bowling side

for every 2 wickets taken during the first 85 overs of the innings, i.e. if they bowl their opponents out in 85 overs they receive 5 points.

The Covering of Pitches

(*a*) The whole pitch must be covered the night before the match and, if necessary, until the first ball is bowled. It can also be covered, of course, any number of days before the match starts.

(*b*) The bowling ends may be covered to a distance of 4 feet in front of the popping creases:

(i) On each night of the match and, if necessary, over the week-end.
(ii) If, during the hours of play, the match is suspended.

Declarations

In all first-class matches a Captain may forfeit his innings and the interval between innings will then be the usual ten minutes. But he must let the opposing Captain and the Umpires know in sufficient time to allow for seven minutes rolling of the pitch.

Drying

If both captains agree, mats or blankets may be used in the vicinity of the pitch in wet weather to enable play to start earlier. These mats and blankets may remain on the ground while play is in progress.

County Championship Matches

County Championship matches last for three days and the standard hours of play are as follows:

First and second days—11.30 am to 6.30 pm (September: 11 am to 6 pm). Third day—11 am to 5.30 pm with an extra 30 minutes on this day on the demand of either Captain in an attempt to obtain a definite result.

These times are frequently altered at most of the grounds, but the following rules have to be kept:

(*a*) No match must last longer than 21 hours or less than 20 hours, including all intervals, stoppages, and extra time.

(*b*) Eight hours (including extra time) is the maximum playing time for any day except Tuesdays and Fridays, when it is 7 hours, except in the case of rule (*f*) below.

(*c*) On no day may play start before 11 am and it must finish by 7.30 pm on the first two days and by 6.30 pm on Tuesdays and Fridays.

(*d*) No match may be scheduled to finish before 4.30 pm (including extra time).

(e) There can be 30 minutes extra at the end of the first and/or second day if both Captains think it might bring about a definite result on either or both of those days. If they disagree, the Umpires decide. Once started, this extra 30 minutes must be played out. Either Captain can still demand an extra 30 minutes on the last day when there is 1 hour left for play (including extra time).

(f) On the last day when there is 1 hour left for play (including extra time), play must continue for a minimum of 20 overs or 1 hour, which-ever is the longer period (provided the game is not finished earlier). If during this last hour play is interrupted by rain, bad light, etc., the number of overs to be bowled is reduced in proportion to the time lost. The basis of calculation is one over less for every 3 minutes or part of 3 minutes which is lost.

(g) The over in progress at the close of play on the final day of the match will be completed at the request of either Captain even if a wicket falls after the scheduled finishing time has been reached. If, however, during this last over the players leave the field for any reason such as bad light or rain there will be no resumption of play and the match is regarded as finished.

(h) On the final day of a match, if a batsman is out off the last ball of an over when less than 2 minutes remain for play, the next batsman must come in and another over must still be bowled.

(i) To decide whether there is time for another over before an interval or close of play the Square Leg Umpire walks at his normal pace to his position behind the stumps at the bowler's end and then checks with the clock which has been selected as the official time-piece before the start of the match.

Fitness of Pitch, Ground, Weather, and Light

For Test matches and all other first-class matches the fitness of the pitch and ground before and during play, and the fitness of the weather and light for play are now all matters for the Umpires to decide. But if both Captains wish to start or continue when the Umpires consider conditions are unfit, then play will go on. Similarly, if the batting side wish to continue after the Umpires have judged the light too bad, they may do so. This means, therefore, that there are now no more appeals against the light.

Intervals

(a) *The lunch interval.* This is normally taken from 1.30 to 2.10 pm, but the time can be varied in both Test and first-class cricket if, due to the weather or state of the ground, an alteration is agreed upon by the Captains or ordered by the Umpires.

The interval is still limited to 40 minutes if an innings ends within 10 minutes of the scheduled start of the interval, i.e. if an innings closes at 1.20 pm play will resume at 2 pm.

(b) *The tea interval.* Tea is taken at 4.15 pm in a match in which the drawing of stumps has been fixed for 6.30 pm unless:

(i) Nine wickets are down, in which case play continues until the end of the innings. However, if the two batsmen are still together at 4.45 pm, tea is taken then.

(ii) An innings ends or play is suspended at or after 3.45 pm, in which case tea is taken, and the interval is combined with the 10 minutes interval between innings, but limited to 20 minutes in all.

(iii) An innings ends before 3.45 pm or the game is resumed after a stoppage, in which case tea is taken after 50 minutes play or at 4.15, whichever is the later.

Summed up, this means that if an innings ends after 3.15 pm but before 3.45 pm, tea will be taken 1 hour after the end of the innings. If the drawing of stumps has been agreed for 7 pm or later, all the above timings are 15 minutes later.

There is no tea interval if:

(a) Both Captains agree to forego it.
(b) The close of play (excluding extra time) has been fixed at or before 5 pm.
(c) There has been no play at all between 2.45 pm and 3.45 pm.

Table 1
Past County Champions

1864	Surrey	1873	Gloucestershire / Nottinghamshire
1865	Nottinghamshire	1874	Gloucestershire
1866	Middlesex	1875	Nottinghamshire
1867	Yorkshire	1876	Gloucestershire
1868	Nottinghamshire	1877	Gloucestershire
1869	Nottinghamshire / Yorkshire	1878	Undecided
1870	Yorkshire	1879	Nottinghamshire / Lancashire
1871	Nottinghamshire		
1872	Nottinghamshire	1880	Nottinghamshire

1881	Lancashire	1922	Yorkshire
1882 {	Nottinghamshire	1923	Yorkshire
	Lancashire	1924	Yorkshire
1883	Nottinghamshire	1925	Yorkshire
1884	Nottinghamshire	1926	Lancashire
1885	Nottinghamshire	1927	Lancashire
1886	Nottinghamshire	1928	Lancashire
1887	Surrey	1929	Nottinghamshire
1888	Surrey	1930	Lancashire
	Surrey	1931	Yorkshire
1889 {	Lancashire	1932	Yorkshire
	Nottinghamshire	1933	Yorkshire
1890	Surrey	1934	Lancashire
1891	Surrey	1935	Yorkshire
1892	Surrey	1936	Derbyshire
1893	Yorkshire	1937	Yorkshire
1894	Surrey	1938	Yorkshire
1895	Surrey	1939	Yorkshire
1896	Yorkshire	1946	Yorkshire
1897	Lancashire	1947	Middlesex
1898	Yorkshire	1948	Glamorgan
1899	Surrey	1949 {	Middlesex
1900	Yorkshire		Yorkshire
1901	Yorkshire	1950 {	Lancashire
1902	Yorkshire		Surrey
1903	Middlesex	1951	Warwickshire
1904	Lancashire	1952	Surrey
1905	Yorkshire	1953	Surrey
1906	Kent	1954	Surrey
1907	Nottinghamshire	1955	Surrey
1908	Yorkshire	1956	Surrey
1909	Kent	1957	Surrey
1910	Kent	1958	Surrey
1911	Warwickshire	1959	Yorkshire
1912	Yorkshire	1960	Yorkshire
1913	Kent	1961	Hampshire
1914	Surrey	1962	Yorkshire
1919	Yorkshire	1963	Yorkshire
1920	Middlesex	1964	Worcestershire
1921	Middlesex	1965	Worcestershire

1966	Yorkshire	1969	Glamorgan
1967	Yorkshire	1970	Kent
1968	Yorkshire	1971	Surrey

2. The Gillette Cup

The Gillette Cup Competition was started in 1963 with the title of 'The Knock-out Competition', sponsored by the Gillette Safety Razor Co. Ltd. Its title was changed to the Gillette Cup in 1964. It is confined to the seventeen first-class counties and the five leading Minor counties in the previous season (excluding first-class county second XI's). No Minor county has yet beaten a first-class county in the competition.

It has attracted huge crowds ever since it began, and in addition to the sponsored money, has brought in a great deal of extra gate money, especially as county members have to pay admission fees at Gillette Cup

The Gillette Cup.

Matches. A Cup Final at Lord's always takes place on the first Saturday in September and is to cricket what the Cup Final at Wembley is to soccer.

The competition has not only attracted new spectators to cricket but on the whole it has also had a good influence on the players. Fielding and throwing in first-class cricket are now at their highest peak and this is largely due to the extra speed demanded of fielders in 'instant' cricket. Many batsmen, too, have benefited, discovering strokes they never knew they had, though the purists will say, and rightly, that too many of these strokes are of the cross-bat variety. The playing conditions for County Championship and other first-class matches in Great Britain apply, except as shown below:

Duration

The matches consist of one innings per side and each innings is limited to 60 overs. The matches are intended to be completed in one day, but three days will be allocated in the case of weather interference. Matches scheduled to start on Saturday, but not completed on that day, may be continued or, if necessary, started on the Sunday during the hours of 2 pm to 7 pm. Umpires may order extra time until 7.30 pm on the Sunday if, in their opinion, a finish might be obtained that day.

Cup Final only

In the event of the match starting not less than half an hour, or not more than one and a half hours late, owing to weather or the state of the ground, each innings shall be limited to 50 overs. If, however, the start of play is delayed for more than one and a half hours, the 60-over limit shall apply.

Hours of Play

Normal hours are 11 am to 7.30 pm. The Umpires may order extra time, if, in their opinion, a definite result can be obtained on any day.

Intervals

(a) *All rounds except the Final*

Lunch	1 pm to 1.40 pm
Between innings	10 minutes
Tea	of 20 minutes duration and taken at 4.30 pm except in the following circumstances:

(i) If 9 wickets are then down or no more than 6 overs of an innings remain to be bowled, the tea interval will be taken at the end of the innings, or after 30 minutes play, whichever is the earlier.

(ii) If the team batting second commences its innings before 3 pm, tea will be taken after $1\frac{1}{2}$ hours of that innings, provided there is no interruption.

(iii) If between the hours of 3.45 pm and 4.30 pm an innings closes, or play is suspended (this includes a suspension which may be in progress at 3.45 pm) the tea interval of 20 minutes (to include the interval between innings) will then be taken.

(b) *The Cup Final*

Start of play	10.45 am
Lunch	12.45 pm to 1.15 pm
Between innings	10 minutes
Tea	of 15 minutes duration and taken at 4.15 pm. Adjustments can be made to the times of intervals by agreement between the Ground Authority and the two Captains

Covering the Pitch

The pitch will be completely covered throughout the match in the event of rain.

Limitation of overs by any one bowler

No bowler may bowl more than 12 overs in an innings. If, in the Cup Final, the duration of each innings is reduced to 50 overs, no bowler may bowl more than 10 overs in an innings. In the event of a bowler breaking down and being unable to complete an over, the remaining balls will be bowled by another bowler. Such part of an over will count as a full over, but only in so far as each bowler's limit is concerned.

The Result

(a) *A tie*. In the event of a tie the following conditions will apply:

(i) The side losing the smaller number of wickets shall be the winner.

(ii) If both sides are all out, the side with the higher overall scoring rate shall be the winner.

(iii) If the result cannot be decided by conditions (i) or (ii), the winner shall be the side with the higher scoring rate in the first 20 overs of each innings.

(b) *Unfinished match.* If a match remains unfinished after three days, the winner will be the side which has scored the faster in runs per over throughout the innings, provided that at least 20 overs have been bowled at the side batting second. If the scoring rate is the same, the side losing the smaller number of wickets in the first 20 overs of its innings will be the winner.

If, however, at 3 pm on the third day, in the opinion of the Umpires, no definite result seems possible, whatever the weather, the Umpires will order a match of 10 overs each side to be started.

If no play is possible on the first and second days, the Captains, bearing in mind the time remaining, will be empowered to rearrange the number of overs to be bowled by each side with the aim of achieving a result. In the event of the number of overs being rearranged, a minimum of 10 overs for each innings will apply. If, owing to conditions, it is not possible to obtain a result, the two Captains will arrange another match of a minimum of 10 overs each side, to be played within ten days on a ground to be mutually agreed. Such a match may also be played on a Sunday. In the event of the two teams having great difficulty in arranging another match within ten days, the matter shall be referred to the Chairman of the Gillette and Other Competitions Sub-Committee and the Secretary of the TCCB for decision.

Awards

(a) The County winning the Gillette Cricket Cup receives a prize of £1,000, and the losing Finalists £250.

(b) A distinguished ex-cricketer is appointed for every match to select the 'Man of the Match' who receives £100 and a gold medal.

Table 2
Previous Gillette Cup Winners

1963	Sussex	1968	Warwickshire
1964	Sussex	1969	Yorkshire
1965	Yorkshire	1970	Lancashire
1966	Warwickshire	1971	Lancashire
1967	Kent		

3. The John Player League

The John Player League is the 'copy-cat' of the Gillette Cup with slightly different regulations to suit the Sunday hours of play. Full credit for the success of this type of cricket must be given to the International Cavaliers. This was a team made up largely of past and present Test players from all countries, who each Sunday in the early and middle 1960s played one of the counties in a match which was televised by BBC2. All profits went to charity or the players' benefits and large crowds attended the matches in order to see this galaxy of stars all playing together in one side. In addition to these crowds on the grounds, hundreds of thousands of people watched the match through BBC2 and came to like this type of cricket. Counties soon realized that it was a 'money-spinner', so in 1969 John Player and Sons sponsored this new competition, restricted to the seventeen first-class counties. It has been a tremendous success ever since. Playing conditions are as for first-class matches except as shown below:

(*a*) Matches start at 2 pm with a 20-minute tea interval at 4.10 pm or after 40 overs, whichever is the sooner. Close of play is 6.30 pm unless 5 overs or less remain to be bowled, when play can then go on until 6.50 pm.
(*b*) Each team bats for 40 overs, but if the bowling team has failed to bowl 40 overs by 4.10 pm, then its own innings lasts only for the same number of overs as it bowled.
(*c*) Each bowler may bowl a maximum of 8 overs and bowlers' run ups are limited to 15 yards measured from the wicket.
(*d*) If there is any delay at the start or play is abandoned owing to rain or for any other reason, the number of overs per innings will be rearranged so that each side has the same number of overs (the calculation will be based on a rate of 18 overs per hour).
(*e*) Both teams must bat for at least 10 overs if a result is to be obtained, unless, of course, one team is bowled out in less than 10 overs or unless the team batting second scores enough runs to win in less than 10 overs.
(*f*) If, in any match, the team batting second has not had the chance to complete the agreed number of overs and has neither been all out nor passed its opponent's score, the result shall be decided on the average run rate throughout both innings.
(*g*) Points are awarded as follows:

4 points for a win
2 points for a tie
1 point for no result

The John Player League Trophy.

If, at the end of the season, there is a tie at the top of the table, then the winner of the League will be the side with the best run rate per over throughout the season.

(*h*) Prizes for final placings of 1st, 2nd, and 3rd in the League will be as follows:

1st   £2,000
2nd   £1,000
3rd   £500

(i) Each winning side in each match in the League receives £50. This is shared in the event of a 'no result'.

(ii) There is a £1,000 batting jackpot, whereby each six hit in the John Player League gives the batsman making it one share in the £1,000, i.e. should there be 100 sixes hit during the course of a season, each player would receive £10 for each six hit that he has hit. The batsman who hits most sixes in the season receives a bonus of £150.

(iii) Similarly, there is a £1,000 bowling jackpot. Any bowler who takes 4 wickets or more in a match in the John Player League, receives a share in the £1,000 awarded. The bowler with most shares in the season receives a bonus of £150.

Table 3
Past John Player League Winners

1969   Lancashire
1970   Lancashire
1971   Worcestershire

4. The Benson and Hedges Cup

This is a new, limited-overs competition to be sponsored by Benson and Hedges for 1972 and 1973. Five Teams will play each other on five of the first six Saturdays of the season in four Regions—North, Midlands, South, and West. The first two in each Region will then go forward to a quarter final, followed by a semi-final, and a final, which, in 1972, will be played at Lord's on Saturday, July 22nd.

The Regions are divided up as follows:

North	**Midlands**
Derbyshire	Leicestershire
Lancashire	Northamptonshire

Nottinghamshire	Warwickshire
Yorkshire	Worcestershire
Minor Counties (North)	Cambridge University*
South	**West**
Essex	Glamorgan
Kent	Gloucestershire
Middlesex	Hampshire
Surrey	Somerset
Sussex	Minor Counties (South)

The rules and regulations of the new competition are as follows:

Hours of play
Normally 11 am to 6.30 pm but with certain allowances for extension, if it seems possible to obtain a definite result in one day.

Duration
One innings per side with each innings limited to 55 overs. The zonal rounds will be played on Saturdays, but, if not finished, may continue on Monday or Tuesday.

Limitation of overs by any one bowler
Each bowler is limited to a *maximum* of 11 overs, and run-ups will be *unrestricted*.

The awarding of points
The winning team scores 3 points plus 1 additional point if they bowl the opposition 'all out'. An innings declared closed is considered 'all out'. In a no result match each team scores 1 point. In the event of a tie the side taking the greater number of wickets is the winner. If both sides are 'all out' the side with the higher scoring rate is the winner.

Quarter- and semi-finals
These will be played on a knock-out basis on Wednesdays (with Thursdays or Fridays for completion, if necessary).

The Cup Final
To be played at Lord's on a Saturday towards the end of July.

The winners of the competition will receive £2,500, the runners-up £1,250, the losing semi-finalists £625, and the quarter finalists £400. In addition, the winners of all the forty preliminary matches played in the four regions receive £150.

* In 1973 it will be Oxford University.

There is also a £250 award to the 'Team of the Week' during these matches. There are further awards for outstanding individual performances in all matches in the Competition, £25 in the Regional matches, £50 in the quarter finals, £75 in the semi-finals, and £100 in the final.

5. The Minor Counties Championship

This was first formed in 1895 and is made up of counties not considered good enough to be first-class. From time to time counties do apply to enter the County Championship—Devonshire's was the most recent application. But the last county admitted to the County Championship was Glamorgan in 1921. In addition to the question of having the necessary skills, lack of finance plays a big part in preventing counties becoming first-class.

There are twenty-two Minor Counties (including Lancashire, Somerset and Yorkshire Second Elevens) and, since the teams which compete in this Championship do not all play the same number of matches, the positions in the table are decided on an average basis. The games last for two days and 10 points are awarded for a win, 3 points for a first innings lead or 10 points for a first innings lead, when there has been no play on the opening day. A minimum of eight matches must be played and most teams usually play ten or twelve.

6. League Cricket

Matches in these leagues, to be found in the North, Midlands, Scotland, and Wales, are played on Saturdays or Sundays, or in the evenings during mid-week. They are decided either on a time limit or limited over basis. The majority of players are amateurs but many League clubs, especially in Lancashire and the Midlands, normally have one professional in their side—in most cases an ex- or current Test player from overseas.

7. The National Club Knock-out Competition

This competition was started in 1969 by Derrick Robins in conjunction with *The Cricketer*. The winning team receives the Derrick Robins Trophy and £250 for the benefit of the club. In the first year of its existence 350 clubs applied to play in the competition but, in order to complete all the matches by the end of the season, the number of teams had to be restricted to 256, with the early rounds being played on a regional basis to save time and travelling expenses.

In 1970 and 1971 just under 300 clubs were allowed to compete. The matches are played under *Gillette Cup* rules, but with 45 overs instead of 60 and with each bowler restricted to a maximum of 8 overs.

Table 4
National Club Knock-out Competition Past Winners

1969   Hampstead beat Pocklington Pixies at Edgbaston
1970   Cheltenham beat Stockport at Lord's
1971   Blackheath beat Ealing at Lord's

8. The Cricketer Cup for 'Old Boys' Teams

This knock-out competition was started in 1967 when sixteen schools were invited to play. In 1969 a *further* sixteen schools were invited to compete. The same rules for first-class cricket apply except that each side is limited to 55 overs and any one bowler can only bowl a *maximum* of 12 overs. The Final is played at Burton's Court, Chelsea.

Table 5
The Cricketer Cup for 'Old Boys' Teams Past Winners

1967	Repton Pilgrims	1970	Old Wykehamists
1968	Old Malvernians	1971	Old Tonbridgians
1969	Old Brightonians		

9. The Haig National Village Championship

This is a zonal limited over knock-out competition which is to take place for the first time in 1972. A total of 750 villages have entered and the Final will take place at Lord's in the second week of September. The rules of entry are as follows:

(*a*) The village team must be selected from a rural community of not more than 2,500 inhabitants.

(*b*) The village club must be affiliated to its local Cricket Association.

(*c*) The club must take out a year's subscription to *The Cricketer*.

(*d*) There is also a 'Throwing the ball' competition which will take place simultaneously with the knock-out matches and the best thirty throwers will be invited to Lord's on Final Day. In the intervals the competitors will compete against each other to decide who has the best arm in village cricket.

In conclusion, I should also mention the **Single Wicket Competition**, although this is not in existence at the moment. However, one such competition was played at Lord's in the 1960s and the rules are as follows:

(*a*) The Championship is played on a knock-out basis between individuals matched in accordance with a draw made before the event starts.

(b) Each player bats for 8 overs (or until out—whichever is sooner) against his opponent's bowling. The positions are then reversed—his opponent batting while he bowls. The player with the higher score wins and enters the next round.

(c) Each player is supported while bowling, by a normal complement of nine fielders and a wicket-keeper. With the exception that there is only one batsman and one bowler in each innings, normal cricket laws apply. The bowler chooses the end at which the innings will commence and changes ends after each six-ball over. At the beginning of each innings, the bowler chooses a ball from six offered to him, none of which is brand-new.

(d) The batsman must continue any run once he has crossed a white line half-way between the wickets. After making a run (or runs) which leaves him at the bowling end, the batsman must not return to his own wicket until told to by the Umpire at the bowler's end, otherwise he shall be judged to be attempting a further run.

(e) A tie is resolved by playing two extra overs for each side until the match is decided.

5. Test Matches—Six of the Best

Test Matches are played between full members of the International Cricket Conference. The first-ever Test Match was played at Melbourne between Australia and England on March 15th, 16th, 17th, 1877. Since South Africa left the Imperial Cricket Conference in 1961, Tests between them and England, Australia, and New Zealand have been unofficial, but have been included in Test Match records in *Wisden* and all other statistical reference books. In the same way, the matches England played against the Rest of the World in 1970 were *unofficial* Tests, but their records stand so far as *Wisden* and the BBC are concerned.

Test Matches were originally of three days' duration but can in fact be any length of three days or over as agreed between the two countries playing. For instance, in Australia between the wars Tests were played to a finish, others in England have been of four days, and there was a famous timeless Test at Durban in 1939 which ended in a draw after ten days because MCC had to catch the boat home!

Laws and regulations for Test Matches are in general the same as for first-class matches, though the two countries playing may agree to certain amendments the home or host country usually laying down the conditions. For instance, in Australia and New Zealand there is the eight-ball over and on MCC's last tour to South Africa in 1964–65 the follow-on deficit was only 150 runs even though the Tests were of five days' duration. Again when MCC were in the West Indies in 1967–68 there was no limit to the number of fielders allowed *behind* the popping crease on the leg-side.

For the results of Test Matches between the seven countries, see page 160.

Australia *v.* West Indies
Brisbane, 1960

Out of all the Test Matches played there have been many wonderful games. I myself have been lucky to have seen over 150 of them and here are my best six since 1945. With one exception I was present at them all and they are the five which have given me personally the most pleasure. The exception just had to be included. Although, alas, I was not there, I have heard the story of the sensational finish many times from some of those who took part. I refer of course to the only *tie* ever to have happened in Test Cricket—between Australia and the West Indies at Brisbane in 1960. So although it is out of chronological order let's start with this remarkable match.

In view of its *fairy-tale* finish perhaps the most remarkable thing about it was that up to noon on the last day it was just a very good game of cricket which, it seemed, after a hard struggle, Australia would win fairly easily. West Indies won the toss and batted first, making 453 with Sobers scoring a magnificent 132. Australia replied with 505 of which O'Neill made 181—his biggest Test score—supported by Bobbie Simpson with 92. In West Indies' second innings, Alan Davidson, who had taken 5 wickets for Australia in the first innings, again bowled superbly and thanks largely to his taking another 6 wickets West Indies were all out for 284 after half an hour's play on the fifth and final day of the match. This meant that Australia only had to score 233 to win at a rate of about 45 runs per hour—an easy task on paper even though Wes Hall did take a long time to bowl his overs.

They started disastrously, losing Simpson and Harvey for a mere 7 runs, and soon after lunch they were 57 for 5 with O'Neill, McDonald, and Favell all out. A stand of 35 between Mackay and Davidson took the score to 92 for 6 when Mackay was bowled by Ramadhin, and the Australian Captain, Benaud, joined Davidson with only Grout, Meckiff and Kline to come. The odds had swung West Indies' way. At tea, the score was 110 for 6 and Australia needed 123 to win at a run a

Brisbane, 1960—1st Test, Australia v. W. Indies. The run-out of Ian Meckiff, which meant that the match ended in a tie.

minute with 4 wickets in hand—quite possible, but it still looked like a West Indies victory. Davidson and Benaud thought otherwise. They hit the bad balls for 4 and ran like stags between the wickets, turning ones into twos and half runs into quick singles. The game swung completely Australia's way and with 10 minutes to go they needed only 9 runs to win with Davidson and Benaud still going strong. It then looked as if Australia had this first Test in the bag. But now—as they say—read on!

Sobers bowled a ball down the leg-side to Benaud who pushed it for a single—8 to win. Davidson took another run off Sobers and so gave Benaud the strike—7 to win. Another ball pitched on the leg stump and Benaud thought he would pinch another quick run by pushing it wide of Joe Solomon at forward square leg. But as he called for one and ran, Solomon threw in from side-on and hit the stumps with Davidson a yard out at the wicket-keeper's end. So Davidson was run out for his highest score in Test cricket—a fine 80—and Australia with 3 wickets in hand still needed 7 runs to win. Wally Grout came in, played two balls from Sobers and then scored a single off the seventh ball of Sobers' over. Six to win and with Benaud failing to score off the last ball of the over, Grout was left at the striker's end to face Hall in what was certain to be the last over of the match as there were now only 4 minutes to go.

Hall went slowly back to his mark to start his long run—at that time by far the longest in the world. It was obviously essential for Grout to give Benaud the strike and as the first ball struck him somewhere on the body, the ball dropped at his feet and Benaud scampered up the pitch with Grout in considerable pain somehow reaching safety at the other end.

Five to win. Seven balls to go and Hall proceeded to bowl a very fast bumper which Benaud tried to hook for 4 and so level the scores. But the ball hit his glove and he was well caught behind the wicket by Gerry Alexander. Benaud out for a Captain's 52, still 5 runs to make for victory, now only 6 balls left and Ian Meckiff—no great shakes as a batsman—the next man in. He played the first ball without scoring, and missed the second which went through to Alexander standing a long way back. Grout, backing up, called Meckiff and they just managed a bye, with Alexander returning the ball quickly to Hall who threw it at but missed the stumps at the bowler's end. Four runs to win, with 4 balls left. Hall next bowled a good length ball to Grout and it flew off the top edge of his bat to Kanhai at backward square leg. But to the horror of every

West Indian present, Wes Hall following through fast, dashed for the catch himself and missed what would have been an easy enough catch for Kanhai. The batsman had taken one run, so now it was 3 balls to go and 3 runs to win. Meckiff hit the next ball from Hall up in the air over mid-wicket and it looked a certain four and victory for Australia. But the grass in the outfield had not been mown that day and Conrad Hunte ran round the boundary and was able to pick up the ball which stopped a foot or so from the boundary. The batsmen had run two and were going for the third which would win the match, but in one fell swoop, Hunte picked up the ball and threw it 80 yards straight over the top of the stumps to Alexander. Grout flung himself at the crease but he was out— by a cat's whisker.

What a throw! What speed and accuracy. Just imagine the excitement. As the batsmen had run 2, the scores were now level and one run was wanted for victory by Australia with two balls to go. This was Hall's eighteenth over of the innings and he must have been almost dropping. But he tore up to the bowling crease and bowled a fast one on the stumps to Kline who pushed it to forward short leg and ran. Once again Solomon was the fielder and once again—incredible to relate—he picked up and threw down the stumps from side-on with Meckiff just short of the crease. A roar, and up went the Umpire's finger. Possibly the greatest, certainly the most exciting Test Match had finished in a tie and I doubt if any of the twenty-two players would have wished for any other result.

FIRST TEST MATCH

Played at Brisbane, December 9th, 10th, 12th, 13th, and 14th. Match tied.

WEST INDIES

C. C. Hunte	c Benaud b Davidson ...	24	c Simpson b Mackay ...	39
C. W. Smith	c Grout b Davidson ...	7	c O'Neill b Davidson ...	6
R. B. Kanhai	c Grout b Davidson ...	15	c Grout b Davidson ...	54
G. S. Sobers	c Kline b Meckiff	132	b Davidson	14
†F. M. M. Worrell	c Grout b Davidson ...	65	c Grout b Davidson ...	65
J. S. Solomon	hit wkt b Simpson	65	lbw b Simpson	47
P. D. Lashley	c Grout b Kline	19	b Davidson	0
‡F. C. M. Alexander	c Davidson b Kline	60	b Benaud	5
S. Ramadhin	c Harvey b Davidson ...	12	c Harvey b Simpson ...	6
W. W. Hall	st Grout b Kline	50	b Davidson	18
A. L. Valentine	not out	0	not out	7
Extras	(lb 3, w 1)	4	(b 14, lb 7, w 2)	23
Total		453		284

AUSTRALIA

Batsman	First innings	Runs	Second innings	Runs
C. C. McDonald	c Hunte b Sobers	57	b Worrell	16
R. B. Simpson	b Ramadhin	92	c sub b Hall	0
R. N. Harvey	b Valentine	15	c Sobers b Hall	5
N. C. O'Neill	c Valentine b Hall	181	c Alexander b Hall	26
L. E. Favell	run out	45	c Solomon b Hall	7
K. D. Mackay	b Sobers	35	b Ramadhin	28
A. K. Davidson	c Alexander b Hall	44	run out	80
†R. Benaud	lbw b Hall	10	c Alexander b Hall	52
‡A. T. W. Grout	lbw b Hall	4	run out	2
I. W. Meckiff	run out	4	run out	2
L. F. Kline	not out	3	not out	0
Extras	(b 2, lb 8, nb 4, w 1)	15	(b 2, lb 9, nb 3)	14
Total		505		232

BOWLING

AUSTRALIA	O	M	R	W	O	M	R	W
Davidson	30	2	135	5	24·6	4	87	6
Meckiff	18	0	129	1	4	1	19	0
Mackay	3	0	15	0	21	7	52	1
Benaud	24	3	93	0	31	6	69	1
Simpson	8	0	25	1	7	2	18	2
Kline	17·6	6	52	3	4	0	14	0
O'Neill					1	0	2	0
WEST INDIES								
Hall	29·3	1	140	4	17·7	3	63	5
Worrell	30	0	93	0	16	3	41	1
Sobers	32	0	115	2	8	0	30	0
Valentine	24	6	82	1	10	4	27	0
Ramadhin	15	1	60	1	17	3	57	1

FALL OF WICKETS

	WI 1st	A 1st	WI 2nd	A 2nd
1st	23	84	13	1
2nd	42	138	88	7
3rd	65	194	114	49
4th	239	278	127	49
5th	243	381	210	57
6th	283	469	210	92
7th	347	484	241	226
8th	366	489	250	228
9th	452	496	253	232
10th	453	505	284	232

Umpires: C. J. Egar and C. Hoy

England *v.* Australia
The Oval, 1953

Whenever I am asked which is my most memorable moment in Test Cricket I invariably choose the last ball of the Final Test between England and Australia at the Oval in 1953. The first four Tests had all been drawn but in this fifth and Final Test, England, under a professional Captain in Coronation year, won the match and the series and so regained the Ashes which Australia had held since 1934—a period of nineteen years. As you can imagine, there were tremendous scenes of enthusiasm at the end of the game. I shall never forget the sight of Edrich and Compton fighting their way back to the Pavilion through the converging crowd, though in fact it was only possible to follow their progress from their bats held aloft rather like two submarine periscopes.

For the fifth time in the series, Australia's captain, Hassett, won the toss, and England went into the field with an extra bowler—May and Trueman coming in for two batsmen, Watson and Simpson. But in spite of the Oval pitch's reputation for taking spin, Australia left out Benaud and had no genuine spinner in their side, something which later they were to regret.

Right from the start Bedser and Trueman bowled superbly and, helped by two showers which freshened up the pitch, soon had half the Australian side out for 118. But thanks to some splendid big hitting by Ray Lindwall, who made 62, Australia recovered and their last 5 wickets added 157 to give them a total of 275. England batted for 2 overs in the first evening before bad light stopped play. Hutton was nearly out off a bouncer from Lindwall. He snicked it on to his cap which slowed it down so that it dropped short of the slips. But in the process it knocked off his cap, which nearly hit the stumps, when, of course, he would have been out 'hit wicket'.

On the second day—Monday—England fared badly against Lindwall and Johnston, and in spite of a typical 82 from Hutton and a useful 39 from May, they finished with 235 for 7 with Bailey fighting back. Next morning, supported first by Trueman, then by Bedser, Bailey went on to make 64 and thanks to a last wicket partnership of 44 between him and Bedser, England finished 31 runs ahead.

The Oval, 1953—5th Test, England *v*. Australia. Bill Edrich and Denis
Compton struggle back to the pavilion after England had regained the Ashes.

This proved to Hutton that the pitch was growing easier and would no longer help the quicker bowlers. So when Australia went in and had only scored 19 runs, Hutton brought on his famous Surrey spinners, Laker and Lock. From that moment on Australia were in terrible trouble. An hour later they had lost 5 wickets for 61, only 30 runs ahead, thanks to Lock's great accuracy and Laker's spin. Ron Archer with a thrilling 49 tried to hit them out of trouble with a 6 and seven 4s but the innings ended with the score at 162, Lock and Laker taking 5 and 4 wickets respectively. With three possible days and 50 minutes left for play (a sixth day could be used if necessary) England needed only 132 to win. Hutton was run out going for a second run when the score was 24 but at the close of play Edrich and May were still together and England needed only 94 to regain the Ashes.

There was tremendous tension and excitement on that last morning at the Oval and the runs came extremely slowly—only 24 in the first hour. Then, with the score at 88, May was out and in came Denis Compton to join his Middlesex 'twin' Bill Edrich. Slowly they added 35 runs and then at about a quarter to three Hassett conceded defeat by putting himself on to bowl. Four runs were scored off his over so with 5 runs needed he called to his vice-captain, Arthur Morris, to bowl his slow left-arm *chinamen* from the Pavilion End. A single to Edrich, then Compton played the next two balls with exaggerated care—the crowd were on tenterhooks and they shouted encouragement and crowded round the boundary edge waiting to rush on to the field.

Then Morris bowled one of his off-spinners outside the leg stump. I was commentating on television at the time. 'This is it!' I thought, as I saw Compton play his famous sweep. But no! He hit it all right but the ball was magnificently fielded by Alan Davidson at backward short-leg. Loud cheers and groans—the uproar was now continuous. The fifth ball was the same as the previous one—a slow off-break outside the leg stump. This time Compton made no mistake and hit the ball hard down towards the gasholders. Whether it ever got there I don't think anyone knows—ball and fielders were enveloped by the crowd and up in our television box, overcome by excitement and emotion, I was only able to shout hoarsely 'It's the Ashes, it's the Ashes.' By bowling those last five balls, Arthur Morris became the most televised Test bowler ever! From then on they were used as a demonstration film sequence in every TV and Radio shop in the land and were played for hour after hour, day after day. Such is fame!

FIFTH TEST MATCH

At the Oval, August 15th, 17th, 18th, 19th, 20th, and 21st. England won in four days by 8 wickets.

AUSTRALIA

A. L. Hassett	c Evans b Bedser	53	lbw b Laker	10
A. R. Morris	lbw b Bedser	16	lbw b Lock	26
K. R. Miller	lbw b Bailey	1	c Trueman b Laker	0
R. N. Harvey	c Hutton b Trueman	36	b Lock	1
G. B. Hole	c Evans b Trueman	37	lbw b Laker	17
J. H. de Courcy	c Evans b Trueman	5	run out	4
R. G. Archer	c and b Bedser	10	c Edrich b Lock	49
A. K. Davidson	c Edrich b Laker	22	b Lock	21
R. R. Lindwall	c Evans b Trueman	62	c. Compton b Laker	12
G. R. A. Langley	c Edrich b Lock	18	c Trueman b Lock	2
W. A. Johnston	not out	9	not out	6
Extras	(b 4, nb 2)	6	(b 11, lb 3)	14

Total		275		162

ENGLAND

L. Hutton	b Johnston	82	run out	17
W. J. Edrich	lbw b Lindwall	21	not out	55
P. B. H. May	c Archer b Johnston	39	c Davidson b Miller	37
D. C. S. Compton	c Langley b Lindwall	16	not out	22
T. W. Graveney	c Miller b Lindwall	4		
T. E. Bailey	b Archer	64		
T. G. Evans	run out	28		
J. C. Laker	c Langley b Miller	1		
G. A. R. Lock	c Davidson b Lindwall	4		
F. S. Trueman	b Johnston	10		
A. V. Bedser	not out	22		
Extras	(b 9, lb 5, w 1)	15	(lb 1)	1

Total		306	(for 2 wkts)	132

BOWLING

ENGLAND	O	M	R	W	O	M	R	W
Bedser	29	3	88	3	11	2	24	0
Trueman	24·3	3	86	4	2	1	4	0
Bailey	14	3	42	1				
Lock	9	2	19	1	21	9	45	5
Laker	5	0	34	1	16·5	2	75	4
AUSTRALIA								
Lindwall	32	7	70	4	21	5	46	0
Miller	34	12	65	1	11	3	24	1
Johnston	45	16	94	3	29	14	52	0
Davidson	10	1	26	0				
Archer	10·3	2	25	1	1	1	0	0
Hole	11	6	11	0				
Hassett						1	0	4	0
Morris						0·5	0	5	0

FALL OF WICKETS

	A	E	A	E
	1st	1st	2nd	2nd
1st	38	37	23	24
2nd	41	137	59	88
3rd	107	154	60	
4th	107	167	61	
5th	118	170	61	
6th	160	210	85	
7th	160	225	135	
8th	207	237	140	
9th	245	262	144	
10th	275	306	162	

Umpires: D. Davies and F. S. Lee.

West Indies *v.* England
Georgetown, Guyana, 1968

I felt I must include in this book my most agonizing draw, that is a match saved by England after a long-drawn-out struggle when all had seemed lost. An Australian writing a similar book would be sure to pick the Fourth Test *v.* West Indies at Adelaide, 1961, when their last pair, Mackay and Kline, held out for an hour and fifty minutes to draw the match. Two Tests immediately came to my mind. First the Lord's Test of 1953 when England needing 343 to win, lost 3 quick wickets for 12 and with nearly 5 hours left were 73 for 4 when Trevor Bailey joined Willie Watson for their famous backs to the wall stand of 163 for the fifth wicket. This undoubtedly saved England and I well remember the nail-biting tension of that long, hot summer afternoon. But somehow there always seemed *some* hope that England would be able to draw. Unlike the Fifth Test at Georgetown, Guyana, on the MCC Tour of the West Indies in 1967/68. This Test was the climax of a hard, tough, and thrilling series, where England, under Colin Cowdrey, so nearly won the First Test and almost lost the Second after a bottle-throwing and tear-gas riot. After a dull draw in the Third Test England won the Fourth after a sporting declaration from Gary Sobers. So you can imagine that when they came to play the last Test, one up in the series, they were determined not to be beaten whatever happened. And yet how near they came to disaster in a tremendous six-day battle.

West Indies won the toss on a slowish pitch and made 414, Kanhai and Sobers in a 250 partnership scored 150 and 152 respectively, and John Snow claimed 4 wickets. When England batted, Boycott made a typical century and with Cowdrey (59) added 172. But when Lock was joined by Pocock, England were 259 for 8 and it looked as if the series was going to slip from their grasp. Lock, however, hit magnificently and with Pocock defending stubbornly (he was nearly an hour and a half without scoring), they added 109 for the ninth wicket—an English

Georgetown, 1968—5th Test, West Indies *v.* England. Alan Knott demonstrates the importance of footwork as he defends against the spin of Lance Gibbs.

record against West Indies. Lock finished with 89—the highest score of his first-class career—and England's total of 371 meant that they were 43 runs behind.

Except for a brilliant 49 by opening batsman Nurse and another great but more subdued innings of 95 not out by Sobers, the West Indies' batsmen in their second innings couldn't cope with John Snow. In seven balls, after lunch on the fifth day, he dismissed Nurse, Lloyd, and Camacho, and then later came back just before the close to clean-bowl King, Hall, and Gibbs. So Sobers ran out of partners and failed by 5 to score two 100s in the match. West Indies were all out for 264 and England on the last day needed 308 runs to win. Boycott and Edrich got them off to a good start by quickly scoring 30 off the fast bowlers. But then on came Gibbs and Sobers to bowl spin and England collapsed in dramatic fashion, Gibbs taking 4 wickets for 4 runs in 4 overs. Sobers trapped Edrich with his googly, then Boycott, Graveney, Barrington, and d'Oliveira all fell to Gibbs and England were 41 for 5 with just under 4 hours left.

Cowdrey was joined by Knott and although these two had batted superbly throughout the tour, I think every Englishman present at this moment saw only one result—a West Indies' victory and, with it, all Cowdrey's hopes and endeavours crashing to the ground. But somehow he and Knott stayed there against the wiles of Gibbs and Sobers who bowled over 70 overs between them in the innings. In an attempt to flurry the batsmen they got through their overs at a breathless pace, sacrificing somewhat their accuracy and direction in the process. Both batsmen used their pads more than one normally likes to see, but I must admit that at that stage I was prepared for them to do anything to survive, so long as it was legal! However, with 70 minutes still to go Cowdrey was lbw to Gibbs for 82. By a mixture of hitting the bad balls for 4 and keeping out the good balls they had added 127. But 70 minutes was a long time for tail-enders to last against the class spin of Gibbs and Sobers. Snow, who seemed to play *every* ball with his pads lasted 35 minutes before he, like Cowdrey, eventually misjudged the line and was lbw for a sterling 1.

Lock, somewhat desperate, lasted only 8 minutes and Pocock for 10, being unluckily given out 'caught' first bounce. All this time, Knott was defending sternly but hitting anything loose and wide of the stumps for 4—especially with his favourite cut. Pocock was out amidst scenes of unbelievable excitement and shouting from the now frenzied crowd. The last man in, Jeff Jones, had one ball from Gibbs to play and seemed to be in a complete daze. After all, his career batting average in first-class cricket was at that stage 4·09, so you can hardly blame him! Furthermore, he had been sitting watching this tense struggle all day and at close of play the night before could hardly have expected to be called on to play such a vital role! Anyway, with our hearts in our mouths we watched him lunge out with his pads at Gibbs and survive that one ball. Then Knott played an immaculate maiden over from Sobers. There was just time for one more over and the result of the series depended on Jeff Jones.

The shouts from the crowd were deafening and it was impossible to give a fluent and coherent commentary. But somehow—and don't ask me how many times he hit the ball with his bat—Jeff Jones played out that last over, surrounded by the whole of the West Indies side. He might have let the ball hit his bat once but I mustn't exaggerate! But there he was 'not out' at the close of play, and gallant little Alan Knott had batted for nearly $4\frac{1}{2}$ hours for 73 not out, which remarkably contained no fewer than 15 fours, so sure was his defence and so expert his dispatch of any bad ball. It is an innings he will never forget and certainly I don't want to go through such prolonged agony ever again.

FIFTH TEST MATCH
Played at Georgetown, March 28th, 29th, 30th, April 1st, 2nd, and 3rd.
Match drawn.

WEST INDIES

S. M. Nurse	c. Knott b Snow	17	lbw b Snow	49
G. S. Camacho	c and b Jones	14	c Graveney b Snow	26
R. B. Kanhai	c Edrich b Pocock	150	c Edrich b Jones	22
B. F. Butcher	run out	18	c Lock b Pocock	18
†G. S. Sobers	c Cowdrey b Barrington	152	not out	95
C. H. Lloyd	b Lock	31	c Knott b Snow	1
D. A. J. Holford	lbw b Snow	1	b Lock	3
‡D. L. Murray	c Knott b Lock	8	c Boycott b Pocock	16
L. A. King	b Snow	8	b Snow	20
W. W. Hall	not out	5	b Snow	7
L. R. Gibbs	b Snow	1	b Snow	0
Extras	(lb 3, w 2, nb 4)	9	(b 1, lb 2, w 1, nb 3)	7
Total		414		264

ENGLAND

Batsman	1st innings		2nd innings	
G. Boycott	c Murray b Hall	116	b Gibbs	30
J. H. Edrich	c Murray b Sobers	0	c Gibbs b Sobers	6
†M. C. Cowdrey	lbw b Sobers	59	lbw b Gibbs	82
T. W. Graveney	c. Murray b Hall	27	c Murray b Gibbs	0
K. F. Barrington	c Kanhai b Sobers	4	c Lloyd b Gibbs	0
B. L. d'Oliveira	c Nurse b Holford	27	c and b Gibbs	2
‡A. P. E. Knott	lbw b Holford	7	not out	73
J. A. Snow	b Gibbs	0	lbw b Sobers	1
G. A. R. Lock	b King	89	c King b Sobers	2
P. I. Pocock	c and b King	13	c Lloyd b Gibbs	0
I. J. Jones	not out	0	not out	0
Extras	(b 12, lb 14, nb 3)	29	(b 9, w 1)	10
Total		371	(9 wkts)	206

BOWLING

ENGLAND	O	M	R	W	O	M	R	W
Jones	31	5	114	1	17	1	81	1
Snow	27·4	2	82	4	15·2	0	60	6
d'Oliveira	8	1	27	0	8	0	28	0
Pocock	38	11	78	1	17	1	66	2
Barrington	18	4	43	1				
Lock	28	7	61	2	9	1	22	1
WEST INDIES								
Sobers	37	15	72	3	31	16	53	3
Hall	19	3	71	2	13	6	26	0
King	38·2	11	79	2	9	1	11	0
Holford	31	10	54	2	17	9	37	0
Gibbs	33	9	59	1	40	20	60	6
Butcher	5	3	7	0	10	7	9	0

FALL OF WICKETS

	WI 1st	E 1st	WI 2nd	E 2nd
1st	29	13	78	33
2nd	35	185	84	37
3rd	72	185	86	37
4th	322	194	133	39
5th	385	240	171	41
6th	387	252	201	168
7th	399	257	216	198
8th	400	259	252	200
9th	412	368	264	206
10th	414	371	264	

Umpires: C. Jordan and C. Kippins

England *v.* West Indies
Lords, 1963

I shall never forget the dramatic climax of the Second Test at Lord's in 1963 between England and the West Indies. At the BBC it is famous as the Test which stopped the TV News—literally. Because of the tremendous excitement at the finish I was told by our producer to say that we would stay at Lord's and not go over to Alexandra Palace for the usual 5.50 news—something quite unheard of at the BBC where the News is sacred. In fact someone up at Alexandra Palace must have had itchy fingers or perhaps disliked or knew nothing about cricket, for after listening to an over of commentary and not getting the finish they had expected, they quietly faded us out and started the News—only to be swamped by telephone calls from irate viewers, one of whom happened to be the Director of BBC TV himself. So back they hurriedly came and viewers were able to share in one of the most thrilling finishes of all time.

But right from the start the match was a winner—first one side was on top, then the other, and so it went on for five days. England brought back Derek Shackleton at the age of thirty-eight and, captained by Ted Dexter, lost the toss. Frank Worrell chose to bat and Conrad Hunte hit the first three balls of the match off Freddie Trueman for 4 a piece. What a start! Poor Freddie was perhaps handicapped by a slippery run up as rain had delayed the start. But for the rest of the day England were on top. At lunch the West Indies' score was only 47, Shackleton moving the ball all over the place but without any luck. Kanhai played attractively for 73, and Sobers, 42, and Solomon, 56, shared useful stands with him. But at the close of play West Indies were only 245 for 6, 5 of the wickets falling to Trueman, none to the unlucky Shackleton. But he made up for it the next morning, taking 3 wickets in 4 balls to finish off the West Indies' innings for a total of 301.

Then Charlie Griffith struck two early blows for West Indies and with Edrich and Stewart out, England were 20 for 2 when Ken Barrington joined Ted Dexter. There followed a masterful display of power-driving

Lord's 1963—2nd Test, England v. West Indies. Colin Cowdrey's dramatic
appearance with his left wrist in plaster.

and hooking by Ted Dexter. He lashed the fiery fast bowling all over the field. He reached his 50 in 48 minutes and hit ten 4s in 81 minutes off 73 balls before being lbw to Sobers for 70. I give these details because for me this is still the best *short* Test innings I have ever seen. Dexter and Barrington had added 82 in an hour. But Cowdrey and Close failed and it was left to Barrington's 80 and Parks' 35 to help England to 244 for 7 at close of play. The pattern was much the same as the West Indies' innings on the day before. But in spite of a brave 52 not out by Freddie Titmus England were all out for 297 on the Saturday morning, 4 runs behind and with Charlie Griffith finishing with bowling figures of 5 for 91.

At the start of West Indies' second innings the game swung right round once more in England's favour, Trueman and Shackleton dismissing five West Indies' batsmen for 104. Surely England were on top now? Yes, but by the close a fine partnership by Basil Butcher and Frank Worrell took the West Indies' score to 214 for 5—a more than useful lead of 218 in a match where the bowlers were on top of the batsmen. But on Monday morning the see-saw started again and West Indies' innings closed for 229—the last 5 wickets falling for only 15 runs in 6 overs. Butcher made a great 133 and he and Worrell had added 110. Once again Trueman had done most of the damage, taking 5 for 52, giving him 11 for 152 in the match, supported by Shackleton with figures of 4 for 72.

So with just under $11\frac{1}{2}$ hours left to play, England needed 234 to win. Although such a total wouldn't be reached without a fight, there was all the time in the world and at this point English hopes were high. But as happened so often in this match they were soon to be dashed. Stewart, Edrich and Dexter were quickly out and England were 31 for 3, leaving 203 runs still needed when Cowdrey joined Barrington. Hall was bowling very fast and short and the ball was lifting dangerously. The two batsmen stuck it bravely but when he had scored 19, Cowdrey received a cracking blow on the bone just above the left wrist and had to retire hurt.

The score was then 72 and an X-ray revealed that the bone was broken and the wrist was straightaway put into plaster. At that time no one knew whether Cowdrey would be available to resume batting or not, being sufficiently optimistic not to look so far ahead. But in bad light Barrington was playing one of his best Test innings, showing unusual aggression (he hit Gibbs for two 6s in one over) and with Close took the score to 116 for 3 when the light became too bad at 4.45 and play was abandoned for the day.

So England still needed 118 to win with 6 wickets in hand plus Cowdrey to keep one end up, if necessary. But Tuesday was dark and wet, and play could not start until 2.20 pm. So now with Hall and Griffith averaging no more than 14 overs per hour, time suddenly became an important factor, and England's chances were not helped by a very different Barrington from that of the day before. He made only 5 runs in 55 minutes and at the end of the first hour only 16 had been scored, which left 100 needed for victory in a possible 125 minutes. Close and Parks took the score to 158 and at tea the score was 171 for 5 with 63 runs needed in 85 minutes—still perfectly possible, but we kept reminding ourselves that with Cowdrey injured it was really 171 for 6 and that at the rate Hall and Griffith were bowling the run rate needed was at least $3\frac{1}{2}$ runs per over.

After tea Titmus and Trueman fell to successive balls from Hall, and with Allen as his partner Close began to charge down the pitch against the fast bowlers. He was trying to knock them off their length and although he scored some runs on the leg-side, it was too dangerous a tactic to last and he was caught down the leg-side by wicket-keeper Murray. Close had made 70 valuable runs and had batted with great courage, finishing up with his body a mass of bruises. And so with 19 minutes left England were 219 for 8 when Shackleton joined Allen to try and get the 15 runs needed for victory. They managed to sneak 7 of these before Hall paced out his long run back to the Pavilion to start the last over of the match. Six balls left. Eight runs needed. Allen and Shackleton were both *normally* good for 20 or so runs. I say normally because this occasion was far from that. They knew that at a pinch Cowdrey would come out to act as non-striker but (with a broken wrist) could hardly be expected to stand up to the thunderbolts of Hall.

The tension on the ground was unbearable. English supporters in the crowd were hushed; West Indians were shouting encouragement to their heroes—especially big Wes. The eyes and ears of Great Britain were also sharing in the scene through TV and radio. Hall must have had memories of that final over at Brisbane as he set out on his long run. No score off the first ball, 1 run to Shackleton off the second and another to Allen off the third. Frank Worrell, the Captain, was calming and encouraging his side just as he had done at Brisbane, 'Relax fellows, relax.' He, as ever, looked the most relaxed of all as he stood quietly at forward short leg. Six runs were needed and only 3 balls left, so Shackleton clearly had to do something. He pushed the ball in front of him on the leg side and called for a run. The ball went straight to Worrell who, true to his maxim, did not panic. He saw the thirty-eight-year-old Shackleton setting off for the bowler's end and made a quick decision. He wouldn't throw at the stumps—Wes Hall wasn't behind them anyway. He may or may not have remembered that he too was aged thirty-eight. Anyway, he backed himself to outsprint Shackleton and, turning with the ball, *ran* to the bowlers end, knocking off the bails a split second before Shackleton arrived breathless at the crease. So Shackleton was run out and Cowdrey had to come in to join Allen.

Six runs still wanted, 2 balls to go. So in theory any of four results was possible but I don't believe that Allen ever intended to go for the runs. Had he scored an odd number, Cowdrey would have had to face a ball and he later revealed that he would have stood facing the bowler as a left-hander holding the bat with the right hand only. Of course you may ask why Allen didn't try to hit a 6 off the last ball. But be honest. Would you have done so? At all events he played the last 2 balls from Hall with a dead bat and the match was a draw—one of the greatest since cricket began and proof that for a game to be great one side needn't necessarily win. I think that both teams were equally happy to settle for a draw and so too, I think, were the spectators. Both sides deserved to win, but neither one of them to lose.

THE SECOND TEST MATCH
Played at Lord's, June 20th, 21st, 22nd, 24th, and 25th. Match drawn.

WEST INDIES

C. C. Hunte	c Close b Trueman	44	c Cowdrey b Shackleton	7
E. D. A. McMorris	lbw b Trueman	16	c Cowdrey b Trueman	8
G. S. Sobers	c Cowdrey b Allen	42'	c Parks b Trueman	8
R. B. Kanhai	c Edrich b Trueman	73	c Cowdrey b Shackleton	21
B. F. Butcher	c Barrington b Trueman	14	lbw b Shackleton	133
J. S. Solomon	lbw b Shackleton	56	c Stewart b Allen	5
†F. M. M. Worrell	b Trueman	0	c Stewart b Trueman	33
‡D. L. Murray	c Cowdrey b Trueman	20	c Parks b Trueman	2
W. W. Hall	not out	25	c Parks b Trueman	2
C. C. Griffith	c Cowdrey b Shackleton	0	b Shackleton	1
L. R. Gibbs	c Stewart b Shackleton	0	not out	1
Extras	(b 10, lb 1)	11	(b 5, lb 2, nb 1)	8
Total		301		229

ENGLAND

Batsman	1st Innings		2nd Innings	
M. J. Stewart	c Kanhai b Griffith	2	c Solomon b Hall	17
J. H. Edrich	c Murray b Griffith	0	c Murray b Hall	8
†E. R. Dexter	lbw b Sobers	70	b Gibbs	2
K. F. Barrington	c Sobers b Worrell	80	c Murray b Griffith	60
M. C. Cowdrey	b Gibbs	4	not out	19
D. B. Close	c Murray b Griffith	9	c Murray b Griffith	70
‡J. M. Parks	b Worrell	35	lbw b Griffith	17
F. J. Titmus	not out	52	c McMorris b Hall	11
F. S. Trueman	b Hall	10	c Murray b Hall	0
D. A. Allen	lbw b Griffith	2	not out	4
D. Shackleton	b Griffith	8	run out	4
Extras	(b 8, lb 8, nb 9)	25	(b 5, lb 8, nb 3)	16
Total		297	(9 wkts)	228

BOWLING

ENGLAND	O	M	R	W	O	M	R	W
Trueman	44	16	100	6	26	9	52	5
Shackleton	50.2	22	93	3	34	14	72	4
Dexter	20	6	41	0				
Close	9	3	21	0				
Allen	10	3	35	1	21	7	50	1
Titmus					17	3	47	0
WEST INDIES								
Hall	18	2	65	1	40	9	93	4
Griffith	26	6	91	5	30	7	59	3
Sobers	18	4	45	1	4	1	4	0
Gibbs	27	9	59	1	17	7	56	1
Worrell	13	6	12	2				

FALL OF WICKETS

	WI 1st	E 1st	WI 2nd	E 2nd
1st	51	2	15	15
2nd	64	20	15	27
3rd	127	102	64	31
4th	145	115	84	130
5th	219	151	104	158
6th	219	206	214	203
7th	263	235	224	203
8th	297	271	226	219
9th	297	274	228	228
10th	301	297	229	

Umpires: J. S. Buller and W. E. Phillipson.

England v. Australia
The Oval, 1968

My next choice is another Test which England won, thanks largely to the efforts of a volunteer ground staff who made it possible for play to be restarted on the last day when it appeared that a cloudburst had robbed England of a well-deserved victory. This was the Fifth Test against Australia at the Oval in 1968. After losing the First Test, England were robbed of victory by bad weather in at least two of the following three, so that they had to win at the Oval to level the series. Cowdrey won the toss and England made 494 thanks to Edrich (164) and d'Oliveira, who made 158. d'Oliveira had been recalled to the England side at the last moment and until this fine attacking innings he had not been on many people's list for the forthcoming MCC tour of South Africa. The subsequent row which led to the cancellation of the tour is now cricket history.

Lawry was top scorer for Australia in their first innings with 135, but they were all out for 324—170 behind, due to some fine fast bowling by Snow and Brown who each took 3 wickets. But time was slipping away for England—it was already after lunch on the fourth day—and if they wanted to have a chance of winning they had to score runs quickly. This they did—being all out for 181 in 3 hours—all the main batsmen flinging their bats at the ball. Australia therefore needed 352 to win in $6\frac{1}{2}$ hours. That evening they lost both Lawry and Redpath. On the fifth morning the sun was still shining, as it had done throughout the match but there were ominous dark clouds gathering around the Oval. Underwood got Chappell and Walters, and Snow caught Sheahan off Illingworth, Inverarity being the only Australian batsman to show any real confidence. He and Jarman were together at lunch when Australia's score stood at 86 for 5.

With $3\frac{1}{2}$ hours left, it looked odds on an England victory. But during the lunch interval there was a colossal cloudburst. Within half an hour the whole ground was a lake and though the hot sun reappeared at

2.15 pm no one seriously thought there would be any more play in the match. No one, that is, except Colin Cowdrey and the groundsman Ted Warne. Cowdrey *paddled* out to inspect the damage and miraculously the big lake changed slowly into a number of mini-lakes as the water began draining away. Then Ted Warne and his ground staff, supported by a large number of volunteers from the crowd, got to work with blankets, mops, squee-gees, and brooms. Incredible to relate, the Umpires decided play could restart at 4.45 pm, which meant that Australia had to survive for 75 minutes or England take their last 5 wickets in that time. Inverarity and Jarman defended stoutly for 38 minutes. The pitch was

The Oval, 1968—5th Test, England *v.* Australia. A unique picture showing the entire England team within a few yards of the bat appealing for lbw against Inverarity. Charlie Elliott is the Umpire giving him 'Out'.

dead and Cowdrey switched his bowlers from end to end and crowded the batsmen with close fielders—all to no avail.

Then came the breakthrough which England needed. Cowdrey brought on d'Oliveira and in his second over he got a ball to hit Jarman's off-stump as he stretched forward and Australia were 110 for 6 with 35 minutes to go. For the next half an hour we were to watch some of the most gripping cricket which I personally have ever seen. Underwood at once came on in place of d'Oliveira, the fielders crowded even closer round the bat and the pitch which had had hot sun on it for nearly 3 hours began to come to life. Underwood got lift and turn, and batting, though not impossible, must have been a nightmare. Mallett and McKenzie were well caught by Brown at forward short leg in Underwood's first over of his new spell—110 for 7, 110 for 8, and about 25 minutes left. In came Gleeson smiling cheerfully as usual, even in this crisis for his country. He actually shook hands with some of the close fielders as he took up his stance at the wicket! He lasted gallantly for nearly quarter of an hour before being bowled by Underwood.

The score was 120 for 9 as Connolly strode out to join Inverarity with 10 minutes left. Inverarity had been in for 4 hours but only 6 minutes before time his concentration lapsed for once and he played no stroke at a ball from Underwood which didn't turn as much as he expected and struck him on the pad. There was a shout from everyone in the England side—the *farthest* fielder only 10 yards from the batsman. Without hesitation up went Umpire Charlie Elliott's right arm and Inverarity was out for 56 and Australia for 125. England had won on the post by 226 runs. It will look an easy enough victory in the record books but an unsuspecting reader will never know how close it was. England had a lot for which to thank Underwood as he finished with figures of 7 for 50. But there is no doubt that their greatest debt was to the anonymous band of voluntary 'driers-up' who helped Ted Warne and his men to make a playable cricket ground out of a lake.

THE FIFTH TEST MATCH

Played at The Oval, August 22nd, 23rd, 24th, 26th, and 27th. England won by 226 runs.

ENGLAND

J. H. Edrich	b Chappell	164	c Lawry by Mallett	17
C. Milburn	b Connolly	8	c Lawry b Connolly	18
E. R. Dexter	b Gleeson	21	b Connolly	28
†M. C. Cowdrey	lbw b Mallett	16	b Mallett	35
T. W. Graveney	c Redpath b McKenzie	63	run out	12
B. L. d'Oliveira	c Inverarity b Mallett	158	c Gleeson b Connolly	9
‡A. P. E. Knott	c Jarman b Mallett	28	run out	34
R. Illingworth	lbw b Connolly	8	b Gleeson	10
J. A. Snow	run out	4	c Sheahan b Gleeson	13
D. L. Underwood	not out	9	not out	1
D. J. Brown	c Sheahan b Gleeson	2	b Connolly	1
Extras	(b 1, lb 11, w 1)	13	(lb 3)	3
Total		494		181

AUSTRALIA

†W. M. Lawry	c Knott b Snow	135	c Milburn b Brown	4
R. J. Inverarity	c Milburn b Snow	1	lbw b Underwood	56
I. R. Redpath	c Cowdrey b Snow	67	lbw b Underwood	8
I. M. Chappell	c Knott b Brown	10	lbw b Underwood	2
K. D. Walters	c Knott b Brown	5	c Knott b Underwood	1
A. P. Sheahan	b Illingworth	14	c Snow b Illingworth	24
‡B. N. Jarman	st Knott b Illingworth	0	b d'Oliveira	21
G. D. McKenzie	b Brown	12	c Brown b Underwood	0
A. A. Mallett	not out	43	c Brown b Underwood	0
J. W. Gleeson	c Dexter b Underwood	19	b Underwood	5
A. N. Connolly	b Underwood	3	not out	0
Extras	(b 4, lb 7, nb 4)	15	(lb 4)	4
Total		324		125

BOWLING

AUSTRALIA	O	M	R	W	O	M	R	W		FALL OF WICKETS			
McKenzie	40	8	87	1	14	4	14	0		E	A	E	A
Connolly	57	12	127	2	22.4	2	65	4		1st	1st	2nd	2nd
Walters	6	2	17	0					1st	28	7	23	4
Gleeson	41.2	8	109	2	7	2	22	2	2nd	84	136	53	13
Mallett	36	11	87	3	25	4	77	2	3rd	113	151	67	19
Chappell	21	5	54	1					4th	238	161	90	29
ENGLAND									5th	359	185	114	65
Snow	35	12	67	3	11	5	22	0	6th	421	188	126	110
Brown	22	5	63	3	8	3	19	1	7th	458	237	149	110
Illingworth	48	15	87	2	28	18	29	1	8th	468	269	179	110
Underwood	54.3	21	89	2	31.3	19	50	7	9th	489	302	179	120
d'Oliveira	4	2	3	0	5	4	1	1	10th	494	324	181	125

Umpires: C. S. Elliott and A. E. Fagg.

Australia v. England
Sydney, 1971

Commentating on winning the Ashes at the Oval in 1953 is a moment I shall never forget but one which I was lucky enough to be able to repeat when England regained the Ashes in the Seventh Test at Sydney in February 1971. Once again—this time on radio—I was able to describe the final ball which brought the Ashes back to England, so I must include this Final Test also in my selection. Even without that special quality which the Ashes gives to Test Matches this was one of the most tense and closely fought Tests I have ever seen and like all really great games the fortunes of the two sides changed almost hourly throughout the five days.

To the relief of the England camp, Australia dropped Lawry and failed to select McKenzie. Had they played I feel sure the result would have been different. This is not a criticism of their new captain, Ian Chappell, who did a very good job and, on winning the toss, put England in to bat. England were without Boycott who had broken his arm, and on a lively pitch in a humid atmosphere had only scored 11 for 1 wicket at the end of the first hour. Luckhurst, for once, failed. Had McKenzie been bowling he must have taken some wickets. As it was, the inexperienced opening pair of Lillee and Dell bowled too short and were very wild in their direction. Even so, England struggled for most of the day. Edrich made 30 and Fletcher 33, but with d'Oliveira out for 1 they were 69 for 4 when Illingworth came to the wicket to play yet another of his rescue-act innings. Hampshire went for 10, but Knott lasted over an hour for a useful 27. By this time the two spinners Jenner and O'Keeffe were bowling really well. The pitch was taking spin and the innings closed for 184 with Illingworth eighth man out, bowled by Jenner's googly for the top score of 42. Jenner and O'Keeffe each took 3 wickets, and Chappell's gamble had come off in spite of the poor support from his fast bowlers. But Illingworth was luckier with his. Both Snow and Lever took a wicket in the half hour left for play, and at the close Australia were 13 for 2 with both Eastwood and Stackpole out.

There was a hard tussle the next morning and in the 2 hours before lunch Australia added 71 and lost the wickets of *nightwatchman* Marsh and their captain, Ian Chappell. But after lunch Walters and Redpath added 63 in the first hour. Walters led a charmed life, being missed at slip off Underwood and at deep third man by Underwood off Willis. It also looked as if Knott had stumped him when he took a ball in front of the stumps off a mishit from Walters who was out of his crease. But it was great cricket to watch and a fascinating battle between the footwork of Redpath and Walters and the flight and change of pace of Underwood. He got them both in the end, Walters going yards down the pitch only to be stumped and Redpath giving a catch to the bowler when he had made 59. At tea the score was 165 for 6 representing a considerable drop in the scoring rate—only 18 runs coming in the second hour. O'Keeffe was soon out after tea, and with Greg Chappell and Jenner together the new ball was taken. Then followed the famous 'walk-off' incident. I was broadcasting at the time so most of what happened is clear in my mind. For the rest I have checked and double-checked what happened out in the middle. I have set out the facts below so that you can judge for yourself and make up your own mind what *you* would have done had you been the Captain in Illingworth's place—always remembering that you have a chance to sit back and think whereas he had to act on the spur of the moment.

The first 2 overs with the new ball were bowled by Snow and Lever with no suspicion of a bouncer. With the seventh ball of the third over, Snow, however, did bowl a bouncer at Jenner who ducked into it, was hit on the back of the head, collapsed, and had to be carried off. The crowd naturally enough booed and shouted, roaring their disapproval of Snow. While the new batsman Lillee was on his way out to the wicket, Lou Rowan, the Umpire at Snow's end, told Snow that he should not have bowled a bouncer at a low-order batsman like Jenner. Snow became incensed at this and asked Rowan in not too polite a way whose side he thought he was on. Umpire Rowan then seemed to lose his temper and in what appeared to be an emotional decision, promptly warned Snow under Law 46 Note 4 (IV) for persistent bowling of short-pitched balls. Then it was Illingworth's turn to protest at what he considered a wrong interpretation of the Law. How could *one* bouncer come under the heading of persistent? Unfortunately, in the heat of the moment, Illingworth also became annoyed and was seen by thousands on the

ground and tens of thousands on television to wag his finger at Lou
Rowan. Amid a storm of booing—I've seldom heard such a noise on a
cricket ground—Snow completed his over by bowling one ball at Lillee.
He then turned to go off to his position at long leg. When he had got half-
way there some beer cans were thrown in his direction from the small
Paddington Hill to the left of the Noble Stand. Snow turned back and
returned to the square where Illingworth told the Umpires that he would
not go on playing until the field was cleared of the cans. The team sat
down while this was being done by the ground staff. After a few minutes
the ground was clear and Snow set off again for long leg.

I remember saying on the air at the time that I thought the whole
incident was going to end happily as members in the Noble Stand and
people on the hill started to applaud Snow and a man stretched out over
the railings to shake hands with Snow. Snow went up and shook hands
but a tough-looking spectator who had obviously 'had a few' then
grabbed hold of Snow's shirt and started to shake him. This was the
signal for more cans *and* bottles to come hurtling on to the field, nar-
rowly missing Snow. Willis ran up and shouted something to the crowd.
Then Illingworth came up, saw the bottles flying and promptly signalled
to his team to leave the field. The two batsmen and the two Umpires
stayed on the square. Then the two Umpires made their way to the
pavilion—the first time they had left the square since the trouble started.
Rowan made it plain to Illingworth that if he did not continue he would
forfeit the match and an announcement was made that play would be
resumed as soon as the ground had been cleared, not only of the cans and
bottles but also of a number of spectators who had clambered over the
fence. This, in fact, took only 10 minutes and Illingworth led his men
back 13 minutes after leading them off. In the remaining 40 minutes, the
England side somewhat naturally seemed to have lost their zest, and
Chappell and Lillee added 45 runs so that Australia finished the day at
235 for 7—a lead of 51.

That was the incident as I saw it, though it is true to say that opinions
differ about what *exactly* did happen. I said at the time, and I still believe,
that Illingworth was right to lead the side off. Not only was it becoming
dangerous with bottles flying around, but this action so stunned the
crowd that the throwing stopped immediately and play was very soon
restarted. In other similar circumstances in the West Indies, the fielding
side had stayed on the field and play had to be abandoned for the day.
There was, of course, no excuse for Illingworth to argue in such a
demonstrative manner with the Umpire. He has since publicly said he

was sorry he acted as he did and also concedes that he should have gone back to the square and warned the Umpires that he was taking his team off. But he had to make a quick decision and it is surprising that neither Umpire left the square at any time to go to deal with the incident at the trouble spot. Illingworth and Snow have also been criticized for Snow's return to long leg after the first lot of cans had been thrown at him. There are two views about this. As Captain, you either take the peaceful way out and give way to force and threats or you stick to your right to place your fieldsmen where you like. And finally, Snow was criticized for going up to the fence and accepting the proffered handshake. Who can say what the reaction would have been if he hadn't? I apologize for dealing at such length with this unhappy incident and now you must judge for yourselves. Meanwhile, let's get back to the cricket which continued on the Sunday morning.

Lillee was out to the first ball of the day, caught by Knott off Willis, who 2 overs later bowled Greg Chappell behind his legs for a fighting 65. Jenner came in at the fall of the first wicket, showing no after effects from his injury and he made a bright 30 before being last man out, bowled by Lever. Australia were all out for 264, giving them a lead of 80 runs, and in the 70 minutes before lunch, Luckhurst and Edrich put on 60 with the former playing some brilliant strokes. He was out soon after lunch for 59, Fletcher made 20 and by tea England had made very slow progress to reach a score of 130 for 2. Two more wickets—Edrich 57 and Hampshire 24, fell before the close when England were 228 for 4—leading by 149 runs. They owed a lot to d'Oliveira and Illingworth who stayed together for the last hour and a half and added 64. However, next morning, Illingworth was soon lbw to Lillee for 29 and d'Oliveira caught in the slips off Lillee for 47. Only 34 runs came in the first hour—Knott making 15 of them. England had still not anywhere near enough runs. However, Lever and Snow each hit out scoring 17 and 20 respectively, but when England were all out for 302, they had lost their last 6 wickets for only 73 runs—O'Keeffe with 3 more wickets again looking the most dangerous Australian bowler. Australia needed 223 runs to win in $15\frac{1}{2}$ hours (a sixth day could be used if necessary)—an easy enough task most people thought, even though Australia had not got the steadying influence of Lawry.

They made a bad start—Snow yorking Eastwood for 0 in the first over. But then came tragedy for England. Stackpole hit a short ball from Lever high in the direction of long leg. Snow ran in to make the catch but came too far. He turned to try to make the catch before the ball went

Sydney, 1971—7th Test, Australia v. England. Ray Illingworth chaired off by his team after England had regained the Ashes after twelve years.

over the boundary but somehow overbalanced and caught the little finger of his bowling hand in the fence and broke it. He went off in great pain with the bone protruding through the skin—a horrid sight. Umpire Lou Rowan signalled 6 although in fact the ball had hit the fence and had not gone full pitch over it. This was the testing time for England, already without their best batsman and now cruelly robbed of their best bowler.

But Illingworth outwardly remained as calm as usual, though what he was thinking one can well imagine. Were the Ashes going to slip away from him after all? But the team rallied round him magnificently, Lever soon got Ian Chappell for 6, Illingworth himself had Redpath caught for 14 and bowled Stackpole, sweeping, for yet another fine innings of 67. At the close of play, Australia were 123 for 5 with Chappell and Marsh the not-out batsmen. The other wicket to fall had been Walters who again showed his dislike of fast bowling. This time he played an incredible shot—an upper cut—off a short ball from Willis and was caught chest high on the boundary in front of the pavilion at *third man*! So with two days to go if necessary, Australia needed exactly 100 to win and it was really anybody's match, with Australians tending to think England would win, and vice versa.

Once again the England side backed up Illingworth superbly and he himself, in his longest bowling spell of the series, bowled magnificently. Underwood bowled Marsh, hitting desperately across the line, for 16, and the score was 131 for 6. Knott stumped Chappell off Illingworth— 142 for 7, but O'Keeffe put up a stout defence and had been in for nearly an hour when Illingworth brought on d'Oliveira who virtually finished off the match. He dismissed O'Keeffe and Lillee in successive balls and though Dell saved the hat-trick and hung on with Jenner for twelve tense minutes, at 12.37 it was all over and the Ashes were ours. Jenner snicked a ball on to his pads and it flew to Fletcher at silly point who made the catch and the England team made straight for their Captain, Illingworth, and carried him off the field.

England had won by 62 runs and what a wonderful cricket match it had been. It was of course a personal triumph for Illingworth who led his team magnificently in the field, encouraging and sustaining their morale. In addition he had borne the brunt of the bowling after Snow went off and his second innings figures of 20-7–39-3 did much to win the match. But it was also essentially a team effort and I shall always be glad that I was there to share their happiness in their hour of triumph on bringing back the Ashes to England after twelve years.

THE SEVENTH TEST MATCH

Played at Sydney, February 12th, 13th, 14th, 16th, and 17th. England won by 62 runs.

ENGLAND

Batsman	1st innings		2nd innings	
J. H. Edrich	c G. Chappell b Dell	30	c I. Chappell b O'Keeffe	57
B. W. Luckhurst	c Redpath b Walters	0	c Lillee b O'Keeffe	59
K. W. R. Fletcher	c Stackpole b O'Keeffe	33	c Stackpole b Eastwood	20
J. H. Hampshire	c Marsh b Lillee	10	c I. Chappell b O'Keeffe	24
B. L. d'Oliveira	b Dell	1	c I. Chappell b Lillee	47
†R. Illingworth	b Jenner	42	lbw b Lillee	29
‡A. P. E. Knott	c Stackpole b O'Keeffe	27	b Dell	15
J. A. Snow	b Jenner	7	c Stackpole b Dell	20
P. Lever	c Jenner b O'Keeffe	4	c Redpath b Jenner	17
D. L. Underwood	not out	8	c Marsh b Dell	0
R. G. D. Willis	b Jenner	11	not out	2
Extras	(b 4, lb 4, w 1, nb 2)	11	(b 3, lb 3, nb 6)	12
Total		184		302

AUSTRALIA

Batsman	1st innings		2nd innings	
K. H. Eastwood	c Knott b Lever	5	b Snow	0
K. R. Stackpole	b Snow	6	b Illingworth	67
‡R. W. Marsh	c Willis b Lever	4	b Underwood	16
†I. M. Chappell	b Willis	25	c Knott b Lever	6
I. R. Redpath	c and b Underwood	59	c Hampshire b Illingworth	14
K. D. Walters	st Knott b Underwood	42	c d'Oliveira b Willis	1
G. S. Chappell	b Willis	65	st Knott b Illingworth	30
K. J. O'Keeffe	c Knott b Illingworth	3	c sub. b d'Oliveira	12
T. J. Jenner	b Lever	30	c Fletcher b Underwood	4
D. K. Lillee	c Knott b Willis	6	c Hampshire b d'Oliveira	0
A. R. Dell	not out	3	not out	3
Extras	(lb 5, w 1, nb 10)	16	(b 2, nb 5)	7
Total		264		160

BOWLING

AUSTRALIA	O	M	R	W	O	M	R	W
Lillee	13	5	32	1	14	0	43	2
Dell	16	8	32	2	26·7	3	65	3
Walters	4	0	10	1	5	0	18	0
G. Chappell	3	0	9	0				
Jenner	16	3	42	3	21	5	39	1
O'Keeffe	24	8	48	3	26	8	96	3
Eastwood					5	0	21	1
Stackpole					3	1	8	0
ENGLAND								
Snow	18	2	68	1	2	1	7	1
Lever	14·6	3	43	3	12	2	23	1
d'Oliveira	12	3	24	0	5	1	15	2
Willis	12	1	58	3	9	1	32	1
Underwood	16	3	39	2	13·6	5	28	2
Illingworth	11	3	16	1	20	7	39	3
Fletcher					1	0	9	0

FALL OF WICKETS

	E 1st	A 1st	E 2nd	A 2nd
1st	5	11	94	0
2nd	60	13	130	22
3rd	68	32	158	71
4th	69	66	165	82
5th	98	147	234	96
6th	145	162	251	131
7th	156	178	276	142
8th	165	235	298	154
9th	165	239	299	154
10th	184	264	302	160

Umpires: T. F. Brooks and L. P. Rowan.

6. My Twenty-six 'Greats'

Why twenty-six? Because I have been lucky enough to commentate on Test Cricket on Television and Radio for the last twenty-six years without a break. In that time I have seen all the great Test cricketers and owe them a debt of thanks for the enjoyment which they have given me, so making my job such a pleasant one. I have therefore chosen *my* best twenty-six cricketers from this quarter of a century of broadcasting. There are many more I would like to have included—Dexter, Boycott, Tyson, Adcock, Sutcliffe, Reid, Lloyd, to mention only a few. I have arranged my 'batting' order by putting one name against each year. Where possible, I have made the year fit in with something significant in the cricketer's career, e.g. 1947—Compton's Golden Year, 1948—Bradman's last Test, and 1956—Laker's 19 wickets. In the batting records for each player an asterisk denotes a 'Not out' innings, and the 'Career' records are up-to-date up to the end of the 1971 season only.

I leave you to pick your first and second XI's from these twenty-six names. I have tried and given up! The trouble is they were, or are, all **GREAT** in the truest sense of the word.

1946: **WALLY HAMMOND**

Gloucestershire and England
Born June 19th, 1903. Died July 2nd, 1965

Captained England twenty times from 1938 to 1947. Was one of the truly great all-rounders of all time, famous for his classic cover drive and powerful strokes off the back foot—even in defence. His figures speak for themselves but give no indication of the power and authority which raised him head and shoulders above his contemporaries. There was an aura of majesty about the way he 'glided' to the wicket or moved about in the field. A superb fielder with a wonderful eye, he was one of the best slip fielders of all time, pouching even the most difficult catches in an insolent way which made them look easy. He was also a fine medium bowler with pace off the pitch and had he not been a batsman might well have been as good as Maurice Tate.

BATTING

	Innings	Not Out	Highest Score	Runs	Average	Hundreds
Career	1,004	104	336*	50,493	56·10	167
Tests (85)	140	16	336*	7,249	58·45	22

BOWLING

	Balls	Maidens	Runs	Wickets	Average	Best Bowling
Career	—	—	22,385	732	30·58	9 for 23
Tests	7,967	299	3,140	83	37·83	5 for 36

1947: **DENIS COMPTON**

Middlesex and England
Born May 23rd, 1918

The Cavalier of cricket with the dancing feet, unorthodox in attack, but strictly orthodox in defence. An entertainer who charmed with brilliant improvisation. In 1947 he made two records which he still holds—18 hundreds and 3,816 runs in one season. He would dance yards down the pitch to the slow, and sometimes even to the fast bowlers. His favourite scoring strokes—the late chop, the cover drive anywhere from behind point to extra cover, the on-drive, the hook, and his own speciality—the sweep. This sometimes got him out, but it also scored him many hundreds of runs. Also a useful left-arm bowler with his 'Chinaman' and googly, though his length was often sacrificed for spin. He was casual, handsome, forgetful of appointments, usually late, and often used other people's equipment because he had lost or forgotten his own. Must go down on record as being the worst judge of a run of any of the top-class batsmen. To answer his calls was like booking a ticket back to the pavilion. But it is cricketers like him who pull in the crowds, who for their entertainment prefer something different from their normal everyday life—and there was nothing normal about Compton!

BATTING

	Innings	Not Out	Highest Score	Runs	Average	Hundreds
Career	839	88	300	38,942	51·85	123
Tests (78)	131	15	278	5,807	50·06	17

BOWLING

	Balls	Maidens	Runs	Wickets	Average	Best Bowling
Career	—	—	20,018	620	32·28	7 for 36
Tests	2,722	70	1,410	25	56·40	5 for 70

1948: **DON BRADMAN**
New South Wales, South Australia, and Australia
Born August 27th, 1908. Knighted in 1948

The greatest run-making machine *ever* seen in cricket. He had beautiful footwork, a wonderful eye, tremendous powers of concentration, and *all* the strokes. Believed in attacking the bowler from the very first ball and in staying on top throughout the longest innings. A fine judge of a run who ran every one as fast as he could, he enjoyed making big scores and never gave his wicket away. If he had not been bowled second ball for 0 by Hollies in his last Test Innings at the Oval in 1948, he would have had a Test average of 100 or more. He always scored his runs at an amazing rate and at Headingley in 1930 he actually made 309 not out on the first day of the Test. A brilliant fielder anywhere away from the wicket, he was voted by many as the best batsman of all time, though he was never as skilful on a turning wicket as many English batsmen. On the type of pitches he played on he seldom had need to be. He captained Australia twenty-four times. Bradman was tough, unyielding, fair, and as one might expect from a man with such a profound knowledge of cricket, also possessed great strategic sense.

BATTING

	Innings	Not Out	Highest Score	Runs	Average	Hundreds
Career	338	43	452*	28,067	95·14	117
Tests (52)	80	10	334	6,996	99·94	29

1949: **RAY LINDWALL**
New South Wales, Queensland, and Australia
Born October 3rd, 1921

One of the fastest bowlers of all time with a copy-book action and a wonderfully smooth run-up. He had complete command over length and direction and moved the ball very late either into or away from the batsman. With Keith Miller he formed a formidable, fearsome and ferocious opening attack for Australia. He was a fine fielder and a more than useful No. 8 or 9 batsman.

BOWLING

	Balls	Maidens	Runs	Wickets	Average	Best Bowling
Career	—	—	16,962	794	21·36	7 for 20
Tests	13,666	417	5,257	228	23·05	7 for 38

BATTING

	Innings	Not Out	Highest Score	Runs	Average	Hundreds
Career	270	39	134*	5,041	21·82	5
Tests (61)	84	13	118	1,502	21·15	2

1950: **ARTHUR MORRIS**
New South Wales and Australia
Born January 19th, 1922

A left-hander and one of the most stylish opening batsmen ever produced by Australia. Although an opener, thanks to his good footwork he played the spinners even better than he did the fast bowlers. He always liked to attack the bowling. A very friendly and pleasant personality.

BATTING

	Innings	Not Out	Highest Score	Runs	Average	Hundreds
Career	242	15	290	12,489	55·01	46
Tests (46)	79	3	206	3,533	46·48	12

1951: **KEITH MILLER**
Victoria, New South Wales and Australia
Born November 28th, 1919

A dynamic, handsome, debonair crowd-puller and a genuine all-rounder of the highest class. He enjoyed life, and his cricket matched his character. When in form, could drive with great power, but often nearly did the splits when stretching out to slow bowlers. Was a fearsome and devastating fast bowler, who could bowl six different balls in one over, including even a googly or beamer—all of them from a different length of run. For such a jovial character he gave the appearance of hating batsmen and showed them little mercy, though he was never slow to applaud them if they hooked his most terrifying bumper for 6. A deceptively casual slip fielder who seldom dropped a catch.

BATTING

	Innings	Not Out	Highest Score	Runs	Average	Hundreds
Career	326	36	281*	14,183	48·90	41
Tests (55)	87	7	147	2,958	36·97	7

BOWLING

	Balls	Maidens	Runs	Wickets	Average	Best Bowling
Career	—	—	11,080	497	22·29	7 for 12
Tests	10,474	338	3,905	170	22·97	7 for 60

1952: **ALEC BEDSER**
Surrey and England
Born July 4th, 1918

Nicknamed 'big fella', this much loved character was one of the best medium-pace bowlers who ever played cricket. He had a perfect swivel bowling action and bowled an impeccable length and direction, making the ball fizz off the pitch like Maurice Tate had done before him. A master in-swinger, he later learned to bowl what was sometimes an unplayable leg-cutter. He liked his wicket-keepers to stand up close to the stumps to 'give him something to aim at'. Elected Chairman of the England selectors in 1969.

	Balls	Maidens	**BOWLING** Runs	Wickets	Average	*Best* Bowling
Career	—	—	39,281	1,924	20·41	8 for 18
Tests (51)	15,941	572	5,876	236	24·89	7 for 44

1953: **CLYDE WALCOTT**
Barbados, British Guiana and West Indies
Born January 17th, 1926

One of the three 'W's' who dominated West Indian cricket in the fifties. A large man, 6 feet 2 inches tall, he hit the ball tremendously hard and there was never much competition to field in front of the wicket when he was on the attack. Being a good hooker and cutter he was particularly severe on anything pitched short. Kept wicket or fielded at slip and also bowled medium-paced swingers.

BATTING

	Innings	Not Out	Highest Score	Runs	Average	Hundreds
Career	238	29	314*	11,820	56·55	40
Tests (44)	74	7	220	3,798	56·68	15

BOWLING

	Balls	Maidens	Runs	Wickets	Average	Best Bowling
Career	—	—	1,269	35	36·25	5 for 41
Tests	1,194	72	408	11	37·09	3 for 50

1954: **EVERTON WEEKES**

Barbados and West Indies
Born February 26th, 1925

The second of the three 'W's'. A magnificent stroke player who believed
in attacking and at the same time turned out the runs like a sausage
machine. Once scored five Test hundreds in succession, and was run out
for 90 going for the sixth. A brilliant fielder anywhere.

BATTING

	Innings	Not Out	Highest Score	Runs	Average	Hundreds
Career	241	24	304*	12,010	52·90	36
Tests (48)	81	5	207	4,455	58·61	15

1955: **LEN HUTTON**
Yorkshire and England
Born June 23rd, 1916. Knighted in 1956

Until beaten by Gary Sobers in 1958, Hutton held the record Test score of 364 which he made against Australia at the Oval in 1938. He was the first professional to be appointed Captain of England in England. Still holds the record of the most runs made in one month—1,294 in June 1949. Had a wonderful technique allied with a phlegmatic temperament. He had to withstand a terrible battering from Lindwall and Miller at a time when England's batting depended largely upon his success. Although he injured his right arm in the war so that it was shorter than his left, he was a model for schoolboys to copy with an exquisite off-drive. He could be criticized for not using his feet to the slow bowlers, preferring to play them from the crease. His answer could be, 'Well, look at my record,' and one must admit that the method he used certainly seemed to suit him. Most definitely qualifies as one of the best opening batsmen of all time. As a Captain he won back the Ashes for England and never lost a series against another country. A true Yorkshireman, he hated the enemy and played hard to win or at least to avoid defeat. Sometimes used tactics, which although within the laws, spoiled the game as a spectacle—e.g. deliberately engineering a slow over rate.

BATTING

	Innings	Not Out	Highest Score	Runs	Average	Hundreds
Career	814	91	364	40,140	55·51	129
Tests (79)	138	15	364	6,971	56·67	19

1956: **JIM LAKER**
Surrey, Essex, and England
Born February 9th, 1922

Will always be remembered for the incredible feat of taking 19 wickets in the Fourth Test against Australia at Old Trafford in 1956. It was so incredible that it must surely always remain a Test Match record. His total, too, of 46 wickets during that series is another England v. Australia record likely to stand. Admittedly, at Old Trafford the pitch helped him but that other great spinner, Tony Lock, bowled 69 overs in the match compared with Laker's 68 and yet only managed to take 1 wicket. Like most classic bowlers, Laker had the perfect action with his arm, so high that it used to brush his right ear. He had everything—flight, spin, accuracy, and direction. He perfected the away 'floater' so that unsuspecting batsmen played for the off-break that never was and were often caught in the slips or behind the stumps. He was no mean batsman either, with a Test highest of 63, and he was also a safe catcher in the gully.

| | BOWLING | | | | | *Best* |
	Balls	*Maidens*	*Runs*	*Wickets*	*Average*	*Bowling*
Career	—	—	35,789	1,944	18·40	10 for 53
Tests (46)	12,009	673	4,099	193	21·23	10 for 53

1957: **PETER MAY**
Surrey and England
Born December 31st, 1929

Captained England forty-one times—more than any other Test Captain.
Stands very high up on the world list of top-class batsmen and had a
wonderful defensive technique and fine attacking strokes, especially his
classical on-drive. Hit a 100 in his first Test for England at the age of
twenty-one and from then on, whenever he was playing, the other
England batsmen, however good, seemed to bat in his shadow. Off the
field he was quiet, shy, sensitive, but friendly. On it he was tough, played
hard, and conceded nothing. Without quite being able to pinpoint the
reason I place him in a class above all his contemporaries.

BATTING

	Innings	Not Out	Highest Score	Runs	Average	Hundreds
Career	618	77	285*	27,592	51·00	85
Tests (66)	106	9	285*	4,537	46·77	13

1958: **GODFREY EVANS**
Kent and England
Born August 18th, 1920

Played in more Tests than anyone except Cowdrey and his 219 wickets are a record in wicket-keeping. Full of tireless energy, he was brilliant behind the stumps, and even at the end of the hottest day still walked as smartly between the wickets with his perky little steps as he had done at the end of the first over. He was essentially a showman, spectacular and acrobatic, hurling himself to make catches that no one else would even have attempted. Loved standing up to the faster bowlers and his taking of Alec Bedser's in-swinger outside the leg stump was a sight never to be forgotten. He was full of guts and kept the whole side and even his opponents cheerful! By running out to meet the returns he always did his best to make a mediocre throw look good. Had the occasional off-day and when he did it was a really bad one, e.g. the second innings of the 1948 Headingley Test when Australia made 404 to win in the fourth innings. But between 1946 and 1959 an England XI without Evans never looked the same and in fact, except for two Tests in South Africa in 1948–49, I cannot ever remember his being left out except for injury. As a batsman he always enjoyed himself, taking the cheekiest of singles, either hitting out at almost every ball, (Lords, 1952 v. India—98 before lunch) or defending as if his life depended on it (Adelaide, 1947, where he was 95 minutes at the wicket without scoring). He scored two Test hundreds. If there were more cricketers like Evans, the crowds would flock back to the grounds. Off the field he was a cheerful extrovert, always the life and soul of every party.

BATTING

	Innings	Not Out	Highest Score	Runs	Average	Hundreds
Career	753	52	144	14,882	21·22	7
Tests (91)	133	14	104	2,439	20·49	2

WICKET-KEEPING

Career	1,060 dismissals (811 caught, 249 stumped)
Tests	219 dismissals (173 caught, 46 stumped)

1959: **WALLY GROUT**
Queensland and Australia
Born March 30th, 1927. Died November 9th, 1968

With his gruff nasal voice and tough agressive exterior, Grout was
typical of the old-style Australian cricketer. He always played to win,
being a wonderful team man and a great help to his Captain. Underneath
it all he had a dry and often caustic sense of humour with a good
command of language! He was aged thirty before he kept wicket for
Australia but soon made up for his late start by getting 187 victims over
a span of eight years. Remembered by most people for his remarkable
catches off fast bowlers like Davidson and McKenzie. But to the con-
noisseur he was as quick as any stumper since the war and his work
close to the stumps in 'reading' spinners like Benaud was a joy to watch.
He could hit the ball hard on the leg-side and his top Test score was 74
against England at Melbourne in 1959. When he died of a heart attack in
1968 the Test scene seemed empty without him.

BATTING

	Innings	Not Out	Highest Score	Runs	Average	Hundreds
Career	253	24	119	5,167	22·56	3
Tests (51)	67	8	74	890	15·08	—

WICKET-KEEPING

Career	586 dismissals (472 caught, 114 stumped)
Tests	187 dismissals (163 caught, 24 stumped)

1960: **FRANK WORRELL**

Barbados, Jamaica, and West Indies
Born August 1st, 1924. Knighted 1964. Died March 13th, 1967

A fine all-round cricketer, Worrell will be best remembered for his magnificent captaincy of the West Indies between 1960–1963 when he welded the different islanders into a real team representing West Indies. He was a born leader, dignified, calm, unflappable and firm. He was friendly and charming *off* the field, though *on* it he played hard to win. But he was always fair and his opponents respected him as much as did his own side. His early death at the age of forty-two was a sad loss for West Indian cricket. It was thanks to his soothing influence that the West Indies brought off that remarkable tie against Australia at Brisbane. As a right-hand batsman he was more orthodox but not as exciting as the other two 'W's'. He played straight with a copy book off-drive and a superb late cut. As a left-arm bowler he varied from fast medium to slow— a forerunner of Sobers, although his slow bowling was orthodox left arm.

BATTING

	Innings	Not Out	Highest Score	Runs	Average	Hundreds
Career	326	49	308*	15,025	54·24	39
Tests (51)	87	9	261	3,860	49·48	9

BOWLING

	Balls	Maidens	Runs	Wickets	Average	Best Bowling
Career	—	—	10,116	349	28·86	7 for 70
Tests	7,147	275	2,673	69	38·73	7 for 70

1961: **RICHIE BENAUD**

New South Wales and Australia
Born October 6th, 1930

Started his Test life as a useful leg-bowler and batsman who drove the ball fiercely. He finished his career as a genuine Test all-rounder (the first Test cricketer to score 2,000 runs and take 200 wickets). He was also one of the ablest and astutest Captains Australia has ever had. He lead them twenty-eight times in six series between 1958 and 1963, won five and drew the other one. A fine leader who encouraged his players to such an extent that he was even prepared to hug them if they took a good catch! A profound student of the game he was able to diagnose the strengths and weaknesses of the opposition. Was always prepared to play attacking cricket if the other side played ball, but if they did not he could be as defensive as any Captain. But, owing to his excellent sense of public relations, it was usually the other Captain who got the blame!

He had a nice high action and, especially in Australia, South Africa, and the West Indies, got a lot of bounce out of the pitches. In England he was never such a threat to batsmen except for his 6 for 70 bowling round the wicket into the rough at Old Trafford in 1961. He was not a big spinner of the ball, but flighted it well. He bowled every variety, well disguised—googly, top spinner, and flipper, and could maintain an accurate length for long periods. He was a fine catcher in the gully and his batting grew in maturity until he became a complete batsman, but still with the drive as his strongest stroke.

BATTING

	Innings	Not Out	Highest Score	Runs	Average	Hundreds
Career	365	44	187	11,719	36·50	23
Tests (63)	97	7	122	2,201	24·45	3

BOWLING

	Balls	Maidens	Runs	Wickets	Average	Best Bowling
Career	—	—	23,372	945	24·73	7 for 18
Tests	19,093	805	6,704	248	27·03	7 for 72

1962: **NEIL HARVEY**
Victoria, New South Wales, and Australia
Born October 8th, 1928

A small dapper left-hander with twinkling feet who matched up to the greatest batsmen Australia have ever had. Played more times for Australia than any other player and scored more Test runs than any Australian except Bradman. Essentially an attacking player he nevertheless had a very sound defence and was possibly the best bad wicket player that Australia ever produced. He had all the strokes but was a particularly fine cutter and ran beautifully between the wickets. A fast and brilliant fielder with a nice philosophy about cricket, namely that it was fun and a game to enjoy. When Benaud injured his shoulder in 1961, Harvey led Australia to victory in the Second Test at Lords.

BATTING

	Innings	Not Out	Highest Score	Runs	Average	Hundreds
Career	461	35	231*	21,699	50·92	67
Tests (79)	137	10	205	6,149	48·41	21

1963: **ALAN DAVIDSON**
New South Wales and Australia
Born June 14th, 1929

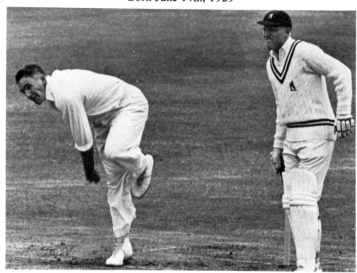

Known as 'Davo', this broad-shouldered all-rounder both batted and bowled left-handed. His bowling was genuinely fast—over the wicket, with the ball going either across the batsman towards the slips, or swinging into him very late. This meant that every ball just outside the off stump had to be played in case it *was* the in-swinger. More often than not it was not and the result was a catch to the slips or wicket-keeper off the outside edge. With the new ball he was devastating and sometimes practically unplayable. He was also a fine forcing bat who really hit the ball and a superb fielder anywhere with a large pair of hands to help him make some astonishing catches. He had to be nursed and encouraged by his Captain, and Benaud was especially adept at this. 'Davo' probably left the field more than any Test player, with some injury or other, which often seemed to the onlooker to be more imaginary than real. But when the crises came, he was quite ready to leap off the massage table and renew battle with the enemy!

BATTING

	Innings	Not Out	Highest Score	Runs	Average	Hundreds
Career	246	39	129	6,790	32·80	9
Tests (44)	61	7	80	1,328	24·59	—

BOWLING

	Balls	Maidens	Runs	Wickets	Average	Best Bowling
Career	—	—	14,052	672	20·91	7 for 31
Tests	11,665	432	3,828	186	20·58	7 for 93

1964: **FREDDIE TRUEMAN**
Yorkshire and England
Born February 6th, 1931

Fiery Fred was one of the greatest characters the game has ever known. A wonderful entertainer, who was loved by crowds all over the world and whose stock of swear words must have rivalled the record number of 307 wickets which he took in Test Matches. He played to the crowd, making ferocious gestures or expressions at the batsman, with his dark forelock hanging over his face. He was a tough, strong, belligerent Yorkshireman with a Rabelaisian wit and an occasional burst of temperament. In his prime he was genuinely fast and had a long curving run with a perfect action. He mostly moved the ball away from the batsmen. Like Keith Miller he could be merciless and hated batsmen, but was quite prepared to applaud a good stroke played off his bowling. He was a very safe catcher close to the wicket and when 'resting' in the deep used to vary things by throwing in left-handed. Could defend stubbornly with a straight bat, when the occasion demanded, but normally his object was to try and hit the ball out of the ground with the crookedest of bats. When he retired, cricket lost some of its colour. There are more stories told about him than any cricketer—some true, some certainly apocryphal—many of them (because of the language difficulty!) being unprintable in a book like this. But one worth telling concerns the time when he came in to bat No. 10 for England in a Test against the West Indies in 1954. Jeff Stollmeyer was the opposing Captain and crowded Freddie with four short legs, a silly mid-off point, gully, and two slips—all the fielders surrounding the stumps with Freddie glowering in the middle of them. 'If you bring any of these b——s in any closer I'll appeal against "flippin light",' said Freddie to Jeff.

	Balls	Maidens	**BOWLING** Runs	Wickets	Average	*Best Bowling*
Career	—	—	42,154	2,304	18·29	8 for 28
Tests (67)	15,178	522	6,625	307	21·57	8 for 31

1965: **BRIAN STATHAM**
Lancashire and England
Born June 16th, 1930

Known as 'George' to his friends and the perfect example of what a
cricket professional should be. Quiet, modest, loyal, completely free
from temperament, and a tremendous trier who would never give up—
the Captain's ideal bowler. Behind his slow Lancashire drawl there lay a
fund of wit and cricket knowledge. Lanky, wiry, and apparently double-
jointed he was also known as the 'greyhound'. He was deceptively fast
with a smooth run-up and brought his arm over high. He was extremely
accurate and bowled straight at the stumps, occasionally moving the ball
off the pitch but seldom in the air. He formed a wonderful partnership
with both Trueman and Tyson and, typically, seemed to play second
fiddle to both of them. Yet without him they would not have been half as
effective. He was an excellent fielder with a splendid arm, and a good
turn of speed. He batted left-handed, and could keep up his end in a
crisis.

| | | | BOWLING | | | *Best* |
	Balls	*Maidens*	*Runs*	*Wickets*	*Average*	*Bowling*
Career	—	—	36,995	2,260	16·36	8 for 34
Tests (70)	16,032	592	6,261	252	24·84	7 for 39

1966: **WES HALL**
Barbados, Queensland, Trinidad and West Indies
Born September 12th, 1937

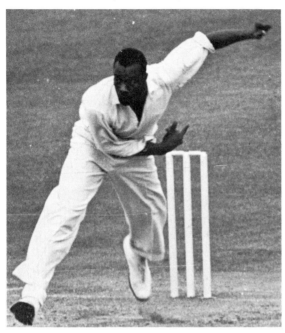

The smiling and, at heart, gentle giant, with possibly the longest run-up of any fast bowler in history. Very fast and unpleasant to play, he relied more on his pace than any particular movement of the ball. His bumpers looked lethal though, luckily, they never were so in fact. Possessed remarkable stamina and could keep up his pace for long periods. A great mimic with a wide range of voices and a marvellous sense of humour he was a favourite with crowds whenever he played, especially when he batted. He rather fancied himself and played some copybook strokes which unfortunately didn't always connect with the ball. With Charlie Griffith he formed yet another fast-bowling partnership to follow in the steps of Gregory and McDonald, Larwood and Voce, Lindwall and Miller, Adcock and Heine, Trueman and Statham. Funny how they go in pairs! He was the bowler concerned in the dramatic last over on two celebrated occasions—the Brisbane tie in 1960 and the Lord's draw of 1963.

			BOWLING			*Best*
	Balls	*Maidens*	*Runs*	*Wickets*	*Average*	*Bowling*
Career	—	—	14,272	546	26·13	7 for 51
Tests (48)	10,415	312	5,066	192	26·38	7 for 69

1967: **COLIN COWDREY**
Kent and England
Born December 24th, 1932

Has played in more Tests than any other cricketer, making the most runs after Gary Sobers, and taking the most catches. Given the initials M.C.C. by his cricket-loving father, he was trained from birth to Captain England and did so twenty-seven times. Although heavily built he is a natural ball player, with an exceptional eye and lightness of foot. He started as a leg-break bowler for Tonbridge at Lord's at the age of thirteen but he soon lost the art and became a batsman in the classical mould. He has all the known strokes plus a sort of sweep of his own, which is really a straight drive in reverse down to long leg. A very good player of fast bowling, he always seems to have plenty of time in which to play the ball—a sure sign of class. Although his figures prove his success, one has the feeling that but for his temperament he *could* have been the greatest batsman of them all. When in the mood he is a class above everyone else, but all too often he appears an ordinary player. The fault lies in his total disbelief in his own ability. Even after 113 Tests he still experiments with new grips on the bat handle or a new stance at the wicket. Nor is his mood consistent. He can start off brilliantly and then for no reason shut up shop. He has made most of his catches at first slip where at his best he could be compared to Hammond or Simpson. As a Captain he can be disappointingly defensive. But on tour in the West Indies he created a real team spirit just as he had done in his fifteen years of captaining Kent, whom he lead to the County Championship in their centenary year 1970. The only player to tour Australia five times, being Vice-Captain on four occasions. Had a very disappointing last tour under Ray Illingworth and just couldn't get going with the bat.

BATTING

	Innings	Not Out	Highest Score	Runs	Average	Hundreds
Career	987	107	307	38,226	43·43	96
Tests (113)	187	15	182	7,700	44·76	22

1968: **GARY SOBERS**

Barbados, South Australia, Nottinghamshire and West Indies
Born July 28th, 1936

The greatest all-rounder the world of cricket has ever seen? Impossible
to judge, of course, without having seen W. G. Grace. But surely no one
can ever have been *better*? He qualifies as one of the first three batsmen
in the world today, possibly the best opening bowler with the new ball
and has no superior as a leg slip. In addition, of course, he bowls
orthodox left arm, or chinamen and googlies. Has now completely
recovered his verve for batting which he lost in the West Indies' tour of
England in 1969, because he was stale and tired from too much continuous cricket. The power of his strokes has to be seen to be believed. He
really hammers the ball instead of just stroking it, and there are few
better sights than one of his sizzling off-drives through extra cover or his
crashing hook to the leg boundary. His movements are those of a giant
cat—he slinks over the ground, light of foot, and his eye and body are in
perfect co-ordination. He holds the highest Test score of 365 not out and
has now passed Colin Cowdrey's total runs in Test cricket with 7,961.
When you ally this to his 226 wickets and 107 catches, can you wonder
that he is described by modern followers of cricket as the greatest ever?
He himself is modest and charming with a delightful sense of humour.
As Captain he is shrewd, if sometimes unorthodox in the field, but he
always plays to win and his declarations, without being give-aways,
usually offer the opposition a good chance if they care to take it. If there
is ever a better cricketer than Gary, I hope I shall be alive to see him.

BATTING

	Innings	Not Out	Highest Score	Runs	Average	Hundreds
Career	513	75	365*	24,715	56·42	76
Tests (86)	151	20	365*	7,961	60·77	26

BOWLING

	Balls	Maidens	Runs	Wickets	Average	Best Bowling
Career	—	—	25,510	928	27·48	9 for 49
Tests	20,322	908	7,531	226	33·32	6 for 21

1969: **EDDIE BARLOW**
Transvaal, Eastern Province, Western Province and South Africa
Born August 12th, 1940

With his spectacles and ample figure Eddie has a look of Billy Bunter about him. But there the fun stops. He is the keenest competitor and most aggressive fighter in Test cricket today. He never gives up and always wants to be in the game, whether opening the batting, snapping up difficult chances at first slip or coming on as first or second change bowler to pick up cheap wickets. As a batsman he is full of guts and unintimidated by the fastest bowlers. In his early days he was apt to slash at the ball outside the off stump and scored quite a few runs over slips' heads. Now he takes fewer risks and makes more runs. He is especially strong off the back foot and a splendid cutter and hooker. As a fast medium bowler swinging the ball away from the bat, he looks a pushover to spectators. But time and time again he has come on in a Test Match when his side badly needed a wicket and has promptly taken 3 wickets in the space of an over or two. He has done this three times in Tests in Australia, twice in South Africa, and again in England for the Rest of the World when at Headingley he took 4 wickets in 5 balls, including the hat-trick. A truly remarkable cricketer, who, because of his character plays far above his natural potential.

BATTING

	Innings	Not Out	Highest Score	Runs	Average	Hundreds
Career	237	13	212	9,655	43·10	27
Tests (35)	66	2	201	2,869	44·82	8

BOWLING

	Balls	Maidens	Runs	Wickets	Average	Best Bowling
Career	—	—	6,586	242	27·21	7 for 26
Tests	3,957	148	1,758	60	29·30	7 for 64

1970: **GRAEME POLLOCK**
Eastern Province and South Africa
Born February 27th, 1944

One of the most exciting batsmen in the world—a left-hander who has often been compared to Frank Woolley. In fact, whereas Woolley stroked the ball away, Pollock power-drives it or crashes it through the covers. He uses a very heavy bat—2 lb 12 oz—and his driving off front or back foot on either side of the wicket is out of this world. He is also a grand cutter and hooker. Early on he appears vulnerable to the ball which leaves him on or just outside his off stump (but what batsman isn't?). Like Hammond he is also said to be weaker off his leg stump. In fact in South Africa the Australians tried to contain him by bowling at his legs to a leg-side field. It certainly stopped his scoring rate but he never looked unhappy. A tall fair-haired giant he has a shambling gait and is basically rather a lazy character. A safe catcher and fielder and also bowls the odd leg-break. A natural at other games, he has recently had trouble with his right eye, and now plays in glasses.

BATTING

	Innings	Not Out	Highest Score	Runs	Average	Hundreds
Career	202	20	274	9,573	52·59	29
Tests (28)	49	4	274	2,506	55·68	8

1971: **BARRY RICHARDS**
Natal, Hampshire, South Australia and South Africa
Born July 21st, 1945

The most technically perfect of all Test batsmen playing today. All his strokes on either side of the wicket, off the front or back foot, are right out of any coaching manual. Unlike most modern batsmen he uses his feet to all bowlers, and advances down the pitch in an insolent way to even the fastest of them—just as George Gunn used to do. He seldom waits to play himself in and if the first ball is a half volley he hits it for a 4. He tends to become careless after a certain time at the crease and one has the feeling that he gets bored unless being fully tested by the highest class bowling. He is ideal for any schoolboy to copy, from his side-on stance at the wicket with his chin tucked into his left shoulder to the way in which he takes up and brings down his bat—in a dead straight line. A very good catcher near the wicket and can turn an off-break quite viciously off a very short run. Definitely one of the few batsmen playing today whom it would be worth travelling half-way across the world to see.

BATTING

	Innings	Not Out	Highest Score	Runs	Average	Hundreds
Career	257	26	356	12,990	56·23	34
Tests (9)	15	1	140	765	54·64	2

I am now going to cheat, and choose one player *in advance*—for 1972. I am really doing this to enable me to include my own favourite cricketer—Alan Knott, known to everyone as 'Knotty'.

They say there are no personalities in the game today. Well, look under the peak of his Kent or England cap and you will see a pair of piercing brown eyes behind which lies a real character. Off the field he is quiet of manner and speech but with each remark accompanied by a wicked twinkle from those eyes. He is fastidious over his dress and takes anything up to two hours to get ready in the morning. He also takes a long time to prepare himself for the field and is meticulous about the cleanliness and efficiency of his equipment. You will usually see him last out of the dressing-room hurriedly pulling on his gloves. He only drinks an occasional glass of wine, does not smoke, likes to go to bed early, and is a fanatic about physical fitness. Many of you will have seen him exercise behind the stumps as he sways sideways, swinging his arms like a gorilla, bending his knees, and touching his toes.

He worries about his health and thinks he is in danger of stiffening up unless he does these exercises. He is also a great believer in pills and takes them as easily as he does a ball on the leg-side. On the field he exudes energy and dynamism and is just like a 'Jack in the Box' as he crouches behind the stumps ready to 'take off' in any direction to make a miraculous catch or save a certain four byes. He is the greatest wicket-keeper in the world today and ranks with the best of all time. Safe, swift, sure, and, at the same time, spectacular, it is inevitable that he is compared with Godfrey Evans.

I have watched them both intently with admiration, disbelief, and, I must admit, with envy. I would say that Knott is more consistent than Evans but through lack of opportunity has yet to prove he is Evans' equal at standing *up* to medium-fast bowling. Evans had to deal with the whiplash of Bedser. Knott only has the gentler deliveries of d'Oliveira. But standing back to the fast bowlers or up to the spinners there is nothing to choose between them. There can surely never have been anyone *better* than either of them. Knott, like Evans, is also a great taker of bad returns and makes the poor thrower look good by going to meet the ball on the full pitch. He also has the same energy and good humour

as Evans did at the end of a long, hot tiring day. Knott has one peculiar-
ity—he finds it easier to take some returns from the field *one*-handed,
plucking the ball out of the air like a conjurer. He makes it look easy but
budding wicket-keepers, please *don't* copy. Knott may do it, but you
may not!

His batting has improved to such an extent that he is now close to
being an England batsman without his wicket-keeping. Like Evans he
can defend or attack, whichever the situation demands. At one time he
found it difficult to play an innings with a mixture of both—it had to be
one or the other. But now he has blossomed out. He always used his feet
well but mostly to defend, picking up most of his runs from the cut. But
now he has become a good driver, even, to the extent of hitting sixes over
mid-off. Knott and Evans have one other thing in common. They are
entertainers who love their cricket and somehow share their enthusiasm
with the crowd. None of us who saw him will ever forget Evans, and
everyone who watches Knott keeping wicket today is seeing a great artist
who, I believe, will become the undisputed master of them all.

BATTING

	Innings	Not Out	Highest Score	Runs	Average	Hundreds
Career	335	63	128*	7,328	26·94	6
Tests (36)	55	9	116	1,655	35·97	2

WICKET-KEEPING

Career	642 dismissals (559 caught, 83 stumped)
Tests (36)	120 dismissals (107 caught, 13 stumped)

7. The Main Techniques

There are many excellent coaching books on cricket written mainly by former Test players. All of them have far better qualifications than myself—a mere commentator—to try to tell young people how to play this wonderful game. I think it would be presumptuous of me to lay down the law about how such and such a stroke should be played or how a ball should be gripped to produce a certain type of swing or spin. Accordingly I have gone unashamedly to what I think is the best of all these coaching books—the *MCC Guide to Better Cricket*. It is authorative, simple to follow, and based on all the right principles. So I commend the next few pages to any of you who want to learn for the first time or merely to check up on your present batting, bowling, fielding or wicket-keeping techniques. If you are able to learn and carry out *all* that it says, in a few years' time you could be a candidate for the England Test Team!

THE BASIS OF BATTING

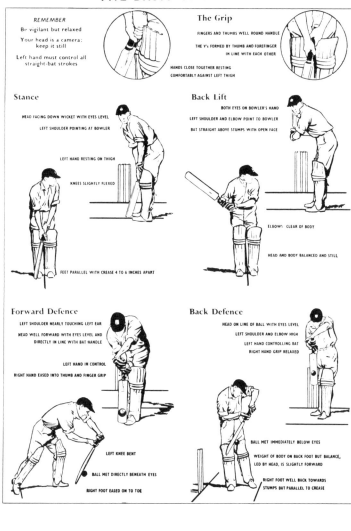

REMEMBER

Be vigilant but relaxed

Your head is a camera: keep it still

Left hand must control all straight-bat strokes

The Grip

FINGERS AND THUMBS WELL ROUND HANDLE

THE V's FORMED BY THUMB AND FOREFINGER IN LINE WITH EACH OTHER

HANDS CLOSE TOGETHER RESTING COMFORTABLY AGAINST LEFT THIGH

Stance

HEAD FACING DOWN WICKET WITH EYES LEVEL

LEFT SHOULDER POINTING AT BOWLER

LEFT HAND RESTING ON THIGH

KNEES SLIGHTLY FLEXED

FEET PARALLEL WITH CREASE 4 TO 6 INCHES APART

Back Lift

BOTH EYES ON BOWLER'S HAND

LEFT SHOULDER AND ELBOW POINT TO BOWLER

BAT STRAIGHT ABOVE STUMPS WITH OPEN FACE

ELBOWS CLEAR OF BODY

HEAD AND BODY BALANCED AND STILL

Forward Defence

LEFT SHOULDER NEARLY TOUCHING LEFT EAR

HEAD WELL FORWARD WITH EYES LEVEL AND DIRECTLY IN LINE WITH BAT HANDLE

LEFT HAND IN CONTROL

RIGHT HAND EASED INTO THUMB AND FINGER GRIP

LEFT KNEE BENT

BALL MET DIRECTLY BENEATH EYES

RIGHT FOOT EASED ON TO TOE

Back Defence

HEAD ON LINE OF BALL WITH EYES LEVEL

LEFT SHOULDER AND ELBOW HIGH

LEFT HAND CONTROLLING BAT

RIGHT HAND GRIP RELAXED

BALL MET IMMEDIATELY BELOW EYES

WEIGHT OF BODY ON BACK FOOT BUT BALANCE, LED BY HEAD, IS SLIGHTLY FORWARD

RIGHT FOOT WELL BACK TOWARDS STUMPS BUT PARALLEL TO CREASE

THE DRIVES

REMEMBER
Get to the pitch of the ball
Keep arc of bat long and flat
Quickness, not strength, gives the power

Off-drive

On-drive

FULL BACK LIFT BAT FACE OPENED

HEAD AND LEFT SHOULDER LEAD
IN DIRECTION OF STROKE

HANDS LEAD
FOLLOW-THROUGH
IN DIRECTION OF STROKE

WEIGHT FULLY ON LEFT
FOOT WHICH POINTS
TO EXTRA COVER

LEFT FOOT AND SHOULDER OPENING
SLIGHTLY TO ALLOW HEAD TO LEAD
ON TO LINE OF STROKE

LEFT SHOULDER
SLIGHTLY DIPPED

HEAD STEADY AND EYES
WATCHING BALL

HANDS HAVE LED A LONG
FLAT SWING

BALL HAS BEEN HIT PAST MID-ON

LEFT ARM CONTROLLING SWING
WEIGHT FORWARD

1   2   3

BACK LIFT   IMPACT   FOLLOW THROUGH
BALL MET CLOSE TO LEFT FOOT
IMMEDIATELY BELOW EYES

Moving out to drive

HIGH BAT LIFT

HEAD AND
LEFT SHOULDER LEADING

LEFT ARM IN CONTROL

I

WEIGHT MOVING FORWARD ON TO LEFT FOOT

RIGHT FOOT HAS GLIDED UP BEHIND LEFT HEEL,
THUS KEEPING BODY SIDEWAYS

HEAD, STILL LEADING, HAS BEEN KEPT STEADY

ARMS WITH HANDS LEADING,
HAVE SWUNG THROUGH
IN DIRECTION BALL HAS GONE

3

LEFT TOE POINTING TOWARDS MID-OFF

CROSS-BAT STROKES

REMEMBER

In all strokes:
  Watch the ball all the way and never lift your head
  Hands lead and right hand climbs over left to keep ball down
In cutting
  Meet the ball at top of rise
In hitting leg balls
  Aim in front of square leg

Cut off back foot

HEAD AND WEIGHT INTO STROKE OVER RIGHT KNEE

HANDS ARE THROWN TOWARDS BALL

BALL MET AT FULL STRETCH OF ARMS, OPPOSITE RIGHT HIP

RIGHT FOOT FACES JUST BEHIND POINT

FULL FOLLOW-THROUGH

WEIGHT STILL LEANS INTO STROKE

Hitting the full pitch to leg

HEAD FORWARD WEIGHT ON LEFT FOOT

BALL MET AT FULL STRETCH OF ARMS WITH HANDS LEADING

LEFT FOOT ON TO LINE OF BALL

The late cut

HEAD AND BODY LEAN INTO LINE OF STROKE

BALL MET LEVEL WITH STUMPS

HANDS LEAD THE DOWNWARD 'STROKE' OF BAT

RIGHT FOOT POINTS TO GULLY

Hitting the long hop to leg

WEIGHT ON RIGHT FOOT WITH BALANCE FORWARD. HEAD ON LINE OF BALL

BALL MET AT FULL STRETCH OF ARMS WITH HANDS LEADING

RIGHT FOOT WELL BACK AND JUST OUTSIDE LINE OF BALL

RIGHT TOE POINTS DOWN PITCH

LEFT FOOT CARRIED AWAY TO OPEN UP BODY

BALL HIT JUST IN FRONT OF SQUARE LEG

RIGHT WRIST TURNS OVER TO KEEP BALL DOWN

WEIGHT NOW ON LEFT FOOT

BOWLING

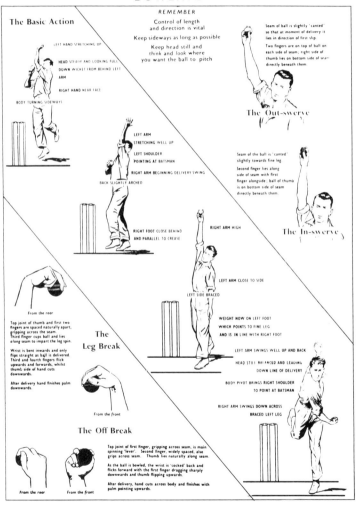

The Basic Action

LEFT HAND STRETCHING UP

HEAD STEADY AND LOOKING FULL
DOWN WICKET FROM BEHIND LEFT
ARM

RIGHT HAND NEAR FACE

BODY TURNING SIDEWAYS

REMEMBER

Control of length
and direction is vital

Keep sideways as long as possible

Keep head still and
think and look where
you want the ball to pitch

Seam of ball is slightly 'canted'
so that at moment of delivery it
lies in direction of first slip

Two fingers are on top of ball on
each side of seam; right side of
thumb lies on bottom side of seam
directly beneath them

The Out-swerve

LEFT ARM

STRETCHING WELL UP

LEFT SHOULDER

POINTING AT BATSMAN

RIGHT ARM BEGINNING DELIVERY SWING

BACK SLIGHTLY ARCHED

Seam of the ball is 'canted'
slightly towards fine leg

Second finger lies along
side of seam with first
finger alongside; ball of thumb
is on bottom side of seam
directly beneath them

RIGHT FOOT CLOSE BEHIND
AND PARALLEL TO CREASE

RIGHT ARM HIGH

The In-swerve

From the rear

Top joint of thumb and first two
fingers are spaced naturally apart,
gripping across the seam.
Third finger cups ball and lies
along seam to impart the leg spin.

Wrist is bent inwards and only
flips straight as ball is delivered.
Third and fourth fingers flick
upwards and forwards, whilst
thumb side of hand cuts
downwards.

After delivery hand finishes palm
downwards.

**The
Leg Break**

LEFT ARM CLOSE TO SIDE

LEFT SIDE BRACED

WEIGHT NOW ON LEFT FOOT
WHICH POINTS TO FINE LEG
AND IS IN LINE WITH RIGHT FOOT

LEFT ARM SWINGS WELL UP AND BACK

HEAD STILL BALANCED AND LEADING
DOWN LINE OF DELIVERY

BODY PIVOT BRINGS RIGHT SHOULDER
TO POINT AT BATSMAN

RIGHT ARM SWINGS DOWN ACROSS
BRACED LEFT LEG

From the front

The Off Break

Top joint of first finger, gripping across seam, is main
spinning 'lever'.   Second finger, widely spaced, also
grips across seam.   Thumb lies naturally along seam.

As the ball is bowled, the wrist is 'cocked' back and
flicks forward with the first finger dragging sharply
downwards and thumb flipping upwards.

After delivery, hand cuts across body and finishes with
palm pointing upwards.

From the rear   *From the front*

FIELDING

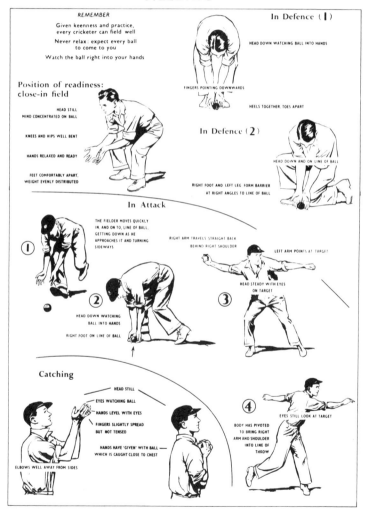

REMEMBER

Given keenness and practice,
every cricketer can field well

Never relax: expect every ball
to come to you

Watch the ball right into your hands

In Defence (1)

HEAD DOWN WATCHING BALL INTO HANDS

FINGERS POINTING DOWNWARDS

HEELS TOGETHER. TOES APART

Position of readiness: close-in field

HEAD STILL
MIND CONCENTRATED ON BALL

KNEES AND HIPS WELL BENT

HANDS RELAXED AND READY

FEET COMFORTABLY APART,
WEIGHT EVENLY DISTRIBUTED

In Defence (2)

HEAD DOWN AND ON LINE OF BALL

RIGHT FOOT AND LEFT LEG FORM BARRIER
AT RIGHT ANGLES TO LINE OF BALL

In Attack

① THE FIELDER MOVES QUICKLY
IN, AND ON TO, LINE OF BALL,
GETTING DOWN AS HE
APPROACHES IT AND TURNING
SIDEWAYS

② HEAD DOWN WATCHING
BALL INTO HANDS

RIGHT FOOT ON LINE OF BALL

RIGHT ARM TRAVELS STRAIGHT BACK
BEHIND RIGHT SHOULDER

LEFT ARM POINTS AT TARGET

③ HEAD STEADY WITH EYES
ON TARGET

Catching

HEAD STILL

EYES WATCHING BALL

HANDS LEVEL WITH EYES

FINGERS SLIGHTLY SPREAD
BUT NOT TENSED

HANDS HAVE 'GIVEN' WITH BALL —
WHICH IS CAUGHT CLOSE TO CHEST

ELBOWS WELL AWAY FROM SIDES

④ EYES STILL LOOK AT TARGET

BODY HAS PIVOTED
TO BRING RIGHT
ARM AND SHOULDER
INTO LINE OF
THROW

WICKET KEEPING

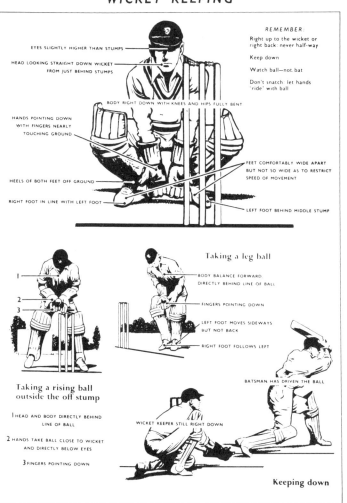

EYES SLIGHTLY HIGHER THAN STUMPS

HEAD LOOKING STRAIGHT DOWN WICKET FROM JUST BEHIND STUMPS

BODY RIGHT DOWN WITH KNEES AND HIPS FULLY BENT

HANDS POINTING DOWN WITH FINGERS NEARLY TOUCHING GROUND

HEELS OF BOTH FEET OFF GROUND

RIGHT FOOT IN LINE WITH LEFT FOOT

FEET COMFORTABLY WIDE APART BUT NOT SO WIDE AS TO RESTRICT SPEED OF MOVEMENT

LEFT FOOT BEHIND MIDDLE STUMP

REMEMBER:

Right up to the wicket or right back: never half-way

Keep down

Watch ball—not bat

Don't snatch: let hands 'ride' with ball

Taking a leg ball

BODY BALANCE FORWARD, DIRECTLY BEHIND LINE OF BALL

FINGERS POINTING DOWN

LEFT FOOT MOVES SIDEWAYS BUT NOT BACK

RIGHT FOOT FOLLOWS LEFT

BATSMAN HAS DRIVEN THE BALL

1
2
3

Taking a rising ball outside the off stump

1 HEAD AND BODY DIRECTLY BEHIND LINE OF BALL

2 HANDS TAKE BALL CLOSE TO WICKET AND DIRECTLY BELOW EYES

3 FINGERS POINTING DOWN

WICKET KEEPER STILL RIGHT DOWN

Keeping down

FIELD PLACING CHART

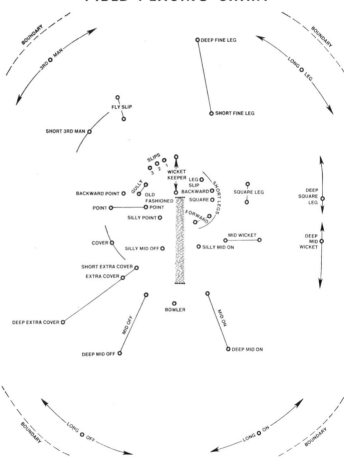

8. Nine Ways of Getting Out

In any game it is important to know and play to the exact laws, and so far as cricket is concerned it is especially important for every player to know when a batsman is 'Out'. The information below, and particularly the diagrams relating to the lbw law should help to clear up any misunderstandings for players, umpires, scorers, and spectators.

(1) Bowled

A batsman is out 'Bowled', if the ball breaks the wicket even if the ball first touches his bat or person. A bail has to *fall* from the top of the stumps. A batsman is 'Not out' if the bail is merely disturbed and not dislodged.

(2) Caught

The striker is out 'Caught', if the ball, from a stroke of the bat or off the hand holding the bat, but not the wrist, be held by a fieldsman before it touch the ground, although it be hugged to the body of the catcher, or be accidentally lodged in his dress. The fieldsman must have both his feet entirely within the playing area at the instant the catch is completed.

(3) Run out

A batsman is out 'Run out' if a fielder breaks the wicket when the batsman is out of his ground while the ball is in play. The batsman nearest to the broken wicket is the one dismissed if they are in the act of running.

If the batsman plays the ball so that it breaks the wicket at the other end, the non-striker, if he is out of his crease, is 'Run out' only if the ball has been touched by a fielder before it breaks the wicket.

(4) LBW

The striker is out 'Leg before wicket' if with any part of his person, except his hand, which is in a straight line between wicket and wicket, even though the point of impact be above the level of the bails, he intercept a ball which has not first touched his bat or hand, and which in the opinion of the Umpire, shall have, or would have, pitched on a straight line from the bowler's wicket to the striker's wicket, or shall have pitched on the off-side of the striker's wicket, provided always that the ball would have hit the wicket.

Should the Umpire be of the opinion that the striker has made no genuine attempt to play the ball with his bat, he shall on appeal, give the striker out lbw if he is satisfied the ball would have hit the stumps even though the ball pitched outside the off stump and even though any interception was also outside the off stump. The diagrams below show clearly when a batsman is 'Out' or 'Not out'.

  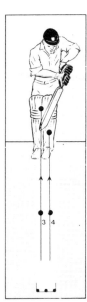 

| Ball 1 NOT OUT as Batsman made a genuine attempt to play the ball with his bat Ball 2—OUT | OUT as Batsman made no genuine attempt to play the ball with his bat | Balls 3 and 4 OUT Ball pitched in straight line between wicket and wicket | Ball 5 NOT OUT Ball pitched outside batsman's leg stump |

(5) Stumped

A batsman may be stumped if he is out of his ground when the wicket-keeper breaks the wicket with the ball in the hand which removes the bails, or if the ball rebound from the wicket-keeper's person on to the stumps.

A wicket-keeper may *not* take the ball in front of the wicket for the purpose of stumping unless the ball has first touched the bat or person of the striker. A batsman *can* be stumped off a wide.

A batsman is out 'Stumped' after *hitting* the ball, providing that no other fielder has touched it, although this used to be recorded as 'Run out'.

(6) Handled the Ball

Either batsman is out 'Handled the ball' if he touches it while in play with his hands, unless this is done at the request of the opposing side. The bowler does not get credit for the wicket and the correct entry in the score book is 'Handled the ball'.

(7) Hit Wicket

A batsman is out 'Hit wicket', if he hits down his wicket with his bat or any part of his person, in the following circumstances: (1) at any time when playing at the ball; (2) in setting off for his first run.

Under this rule: (1) 'Playing at the ball' includes a second strike by the batsman to keep the ball out of his wicket. (2) Any part of the batsman's dress will be considered part of his person. (3) A batsman is 'Not out' if he breaks his wicket in trying to avoid being run out or stumped.

(8) Obstructing the Field

Either batsman can be dismissed 'Obstructing the field' if he *wilfully* obstructs the other side. If the obstruction prevents the ball from being caught, then it is the striker who is out. The only question the Umpire has to ask himself is, 'Was the obstruction wilful?' The bowler in such cases does not get credit for the wicket.

(9) Hit the Ball Twice

A batsman is out if he hits the ball twice, unless the second stroke is made in defence of his wicket. No runs can be scored off his second stroke except from an overthrow. The bowler does *not* get credit for the wicket if a batsman is given out. It is interesting to note that this is one of the four ways in which a batsman can be given 'Out' off a 'No ball', the others being: 'Run out', 'Obstructing the field', and 'Handled the ball'.

'But what about 'Played on',' some of you will say? 'Isn't that a tenth way of getting out?' The answer is a very definite 'No'. 'Played on' is purely a colloquial expression used to describe a batsman's dismissal when he is 'Bowled' after playing the ball with his bat. The correct entry in the score-book is 'Bowled'.

9. A Short Quiz

1. A batsman hits the ball over the bowler's head. The ball hits the sightscreen full pitch. The sightscreen is *on* the boundary line. How many runs does the Umpire signal?

2. Who was the last Englishman to score a hundred on his Test debut?

3. When does the ball cease to be dead?

4. Essex were the only team to dismiss the 1948 Australians in a single day. What was the tourists' total?

5. Who holds the record for the most catches in first-class cricket and how many?

6. How many ways can you be out off a 'No-ball'? Name them.

7. Who has captained England most times in Test Cricket? And how many times?

8. If, while playing the ball, a batsman's cap falls on to the wicket and knocks off the bails, what decision does the Umpire give on appeal?

9. What is the maximum length and width allowed for a cricket bat?

10. Surrey won the County Championship a record number of times in succession. How many times and in what years?

11. How old was Wilfred Rhodes when he played in his last Test for England?

12. In 1932 Hedley Verity created a record by taking 10 wickets in an innings at the least cost? What *was* his analysis?

13. A bowler bowls a bumper and the batsman trying to protect himself flings his bat away. The ball then hits him on his left-hand glove and is taken by short-leg who claims a catch. Is the batsman out?

14. Colin Cowdrey has played in most Tests for England (113). Who has played in most Tests for Australia and how many?

15. What is the penalty if a fielder fields the ball with his cap?

16. How many times have Glamorgan won the County Championship and in which years?

17. How many hundreds did Sir Jack Hobbs score in first-class cricket?

18. Who faced the first ball ever bowled in a Test Match and went on to score the first hundred—165 'Retired hurt'?

19. How many bowlers have taken over 200 wickets in Test Cricket? Name them.

20. Who took the longest time before scoring his first run in a Test innings and how long was it?

21. As a bowler runs up to bowl the first ball of his over he pulls a muscle and has to be carried off without bowling a ball. What action should the Umpire take?

22. Who was the Yorkshire and England Captain who was not born in Yorkshire?

23. Can a batsman be stumped off a wide?

24. Name the Australian bowler who did the hat-trick in each innings of a Test Match *v.* South Africa in the Triangular Tournament of 1912.

25. What is the highest aggregate of runs scored by a batsmen in one season in first-class cricket! Also who scored them and when?

26. If a fielder on the boundary catches the ball with both of his feet grounded *inside* the boundary and then overbalances and falls over the boundary with the ball, is it a catch?

27. When was the last County Championship match begun and finished in a single day?

28. What is the longest innings ever played by a batsman in first-class cricket?

29. Name the counties who have won the Gillette Cup in the nine seasons of its existence?

30. The ball has been hit into the outfield and the two batsmen have just completed one run when a dog runs on to the field, picks up the ball and runs away with it over the boundary. What should the Umpire do?

10. The Tale End

Cricket is fun, not only to play but also to read or talk about. More books on cricket have been written than on any other game. More stories are told about it—many of them true—of events both on and off the field. And behind all these stories laughter is never far away. Few of them are new, but the old ones get reburnished as they are handed down from generation to generation, with the characters sometimes changing. As laughter *is* such a part of cricket, I thought we should end this part of the book with a few samples of cricket humour. If, when you finally put down the book, you have a smile on your face or laughter in your heart, then you will have caught or recaptured some of the true spirit of cricket.

Harold Larwood, the famous Nottinghamshire and England fast bowler of the twenties and thirties, was once staying with a friend in the West Country and went to watch a village cricket match on the Saturday afternoon. The visiting side were one short and Larwood was pressed to play without anyone knowing who he was. As both umpires came from the home side, who were batting, it was proving somewhat difficult to get them out. In desperation, the captain asked Larwood if he could bowl. He said that he would have a try and, taking a short run, sent down an off-spinner, which the batsman missed and which hit him in the middle of both legs right in front of the wicket. 'Not out,' was the reply to the appeal. The next ball, a leg-break, was snicked into the wicket-keeper's hands. Again, 'Not out' was the umpire's decision. Larwood then took his usual run of over twenty yards and sent down a thunderbolt which knocked all three stumps out of the ground. Turning to the umpire he said, 'We very nearly had him that time, didn't we?'

While in Australia with the 1962/63 MCC team David Sheppard came in for more than his fair share of dropped catches. The story was going around that a young English couple who had settled in Australia were due to have their first-born christened. The husband suggested that it would be nice if they got David Sheppard to do it for them. 'Oh no,' said the horrified wife, 'not likely, he would only drop it!'

He was a very slow bowler and had been hit more or less out of sight when at last the batsman missed a ball which pitched straight—like the others it was devoid of spin—and struck him on the pad. The bowler turned round with a howl of triumph to the umpire and cried, 'How's that?' 'Not out,' said the umpire. The bowler was a very well-bred cricketer and it was not until the end of the over, when he had been hit for three more sixes, that he said to the umpire:

'That one pitched straight, didn't it?'

'Yes.'

'It didn't turn did it?'

'No.'

'He didn't touch it, did he?'

'No.'

'Then why wasn't he out?'

'It wasn't going fast enough to dislodge the bails!'

Bill Reeves, the famous umpire, was seldom at a loss for a reply, but he was struck dumb on one occasion as follows:

Surrey were playing Gloucester at Cheltenham, and Alf Gover, Surrey's traditional number eleven, strode to the crease. He took up his stance ready to withstand the onslaught, scorning to take guard. Bill Reeves was never surprised at anything, but noting this somewhat irregular behaviour on Gover's part said, 'Hey, Alf, don't you want your guard?'

'No thanks', said Alf, 'I've played here before.'

In a village match a visiting batsman was hit high on the chest by the local fast bowler—the village blacksmith. To his surprise the bowler appealed for lbw and to his even greater surprise the umpire gave him out. As he passed the umpire on his way back to the pavilion, the batsman said, 'I couldn't possibly have been out, it hit me in the chest.' 'Well,' said the umpire, 'you look in the local *Gazette* next Thursday and you'll see you were out right enough.' 'You look,' snorted the batsman, '*I* am the Editor!'

W. G. Grace was batting on a very windy day, and a fast bowler succeeded in getting one past him which just flicked the bails off. The doctor stood his ground and said to the umpire, 'Windy day today, umpire'. Whereupon the umpire replied, 'Very windy indeed, doctor—mind it doesn't blow your cap off on the way back to the pavilion!'

In a village cricket match a very fat batsman came in to bat, and as he was taking up his stance at the wicket the local umpire confided to the visiting bowler: 'We have a special rule for him. If you hit him in front it's lbw. If you hit him behind it's a wide!'

On the day Fred Price made his record of seven catches for Middlesex in a County Championship innings, he was having a drink in the Tavern after the game, when a lady came up to him and said, 'Oh, Mr Price, I did admire your wicket-keeping today. I was so excited, I nearly fell off the balcony.' 'If you had done so, madam,' he replied, 'on today's form I would have caught you too!'

A fast bowler was bowling on a bad wicket, and the opening batsman —who shall be nameless—had to face a number of terrifying deliveries. The first whizzed past his left ear, the second nearly knocked his cap off, and the third struck him an awful blow over the heart. He collapsed and lay on the ground—then after a minute or two got up and prepared to take strike again. The umpire asked him if he was ready—he replied, 'Yes, but I would like the sight-screen moved.'

'Certainly,' said the umpire. 'Where would you like it?'

The batsman replied, 'About half-way down the wicket between me and the bowler!'

'In a village match a batsman came in wearing only one pad. When this was pointed out to him, the batsman replied, 'Yes, I know, but we only have five pads between us.'

'But,' he was told, 'you've got it on the wrong leg.'

'Oh no,' said the batsman, 'I thought I would be batting at the other end!'

When Frank Tyson was a young man he once went in to bat against a team of first-class cricketers. His form was not very good. He missed the first ball, the next hit him on the pad, he snicked the third, and was clean-bowled by the fourth. As he passed him the umpire said to him, 'Aye, lad, tha was lucky to make nought!'

There is a story about Jack Newman, playing for Hampshire, when he came out to join Lord Tennyson at the wicket in very bad light, and his Lordship called down the wicket to Newman, 'Why don't you appeal against the light, Jack? They won't listen to me.' To which Newman replied, 'I can hear you, my Lord, but I can't see you . . . where are you?'

The Church of England received a challenge to a cricket match at Lord's from the Roman Catholic church. The Archbishop of Canterbury was naturally keen to know what sort of chance his side would have before he took up the challenge, so he conferred with the Rev. David Sheppard, who only recommended acceptance if the C. of E. could obtain the services of Ken Barrington The Archbishop sent for Barrington, specially ordained him, and immediately accepted the challenge.

At half past one on the day of the match he rang up Lord's to ask David Sheppard the score.

'What's our score?'

'I'm sorry, your Grace, but we are forty-four for nine.'

'How dreadful! What happened to the Rev. Kenneth Barrington?'

'Out first ball, I'm afraid.'

'Who is doing all the damage, then?'

'A fellow they've got called Father Trueman!!'

At a Yorkshire v. Lancashire Roses' match at Sheffield, father arrived early and kept a spare seat for his son, who arrived half an hour after the start of play, breathless and pale with excitement.

'Dad,' he said, 'I've got some terrible news for thee—house is on fire.'

'Aye——'

'Mother's been taken to hospital with bad burns——'

'Aye——'

'And she says she forgot to send Insurance money——'

'Aye and I've bad news for thee too—'Utton's out!'

This is a story about the customary annual council match, between Durban and Pietermaritzburg. The Mayor and skipper of Durban had represented his side for fifteen years and, during that period, had only captured 2 wickets and made 17 runs, and had never held a catch. The game was duly played in Durban and after a few wickets had fallen, in strode the Mayor of Pietermaritzburg to take strike. All of a sudden, he took an almighty swing and the ball went soaring into the heavens straight to the Durban skipper. His apprehension was terrific and in the dying moments he closed his eyes and the ball landed safely in his left hand. His jubilation was fantastic—tossing the ball in the air and then lying down and rolling the ball on his forehead—his first catch ever in such class cricket. He then held the ball aloft to receive the congratulations of his team-mates, but was confronted by a rather irate mid-on who said, 'For God's sake throw the ball back—it was a 'No-ball' and the batsmen have run seven already!'

Once, after an appeal for lbw had been turned down, Johnny Wardle, the Yorkshire and England spin bowler, said: 'You know, I think that would have hit the wicket. Where do you think it would have hit?' The umpire (who shall be nameless) replied: 'How should I know? The gentleman's leg was in the way!'

A witch-doctor in Tanganyika had been ill for some time and came to England to see a specialist. While here, he thought he would see whether the magic in England was really better than the magic in his own country. On returning home he was asked by another witch-doctor if he had seen any examples of white magic. 'Yes,' he said, 'I did. One day I went to a big sports stadium where thousands of people had assembled and were sitting in brilliant sunshine. The grass was beautiful and the grandstands were white and gleaming with new paint. I had been sitting there for half an hour enjoying the warm sun, when a man came out of a hut—went to the middle of the grass and put three pieces of wood upright into the ground. He then walked a measured distance and put in three more pieces of wood. I enjoyed the sun for another half hour. And then two men in white coats came out of the hut, walked to the middle of the grass and put some smaller pieces of wood on top of the other six pieces. Then eleven men came out of the hut and spread themselves around the field, and one of them had protective pads on his legs, and big gloves on his hands. A minute or two later two more men came out of the hut, also wearing gloves and pads and carrying pieces of timber. Each went and stood against the three pieces of wood in the ground. Then one of the men in white coats threw a red ball to one of the men in the field. He walked twenty yards away and when he was by himself he began to rub the ball—first on his shirt and then on his trousers. As soon as he did that it began to pour with rain and it went on raining for five hours. What wonderful magic!'

I have purposely concluded with the anecdote about the witch-doctor, not only because it always makes me laugh but because it contains within it one of the elements of true greatness in anything or anybody—the ability to laugh at oneself. This is, of course, yet another instance of what a great game cricket is and fittingly brings this part of the book to a close.

Appendix 1
Answers to Quiz

1. 4.

2. John Hampshire at Lords, England *v*. West Indies in 1969.

3. When the bowler starts his run or bowling action.

4. 721.

5. Frank Woolley—1,011.

6. Four: run-out; hit the ball twice; handled the ball; obstructing the field.

7. Peter May—41 times.

8. Out 'Hit wicket'.

9. 38 inches by $4\frac{1}{4}$ inches.

10. Seven, 1952–58.

11. 52 years 165 days.

12. 10 for 10.

13. No.

14. Neil Harvey—79.

15. Five runs, plus any runs already run.

16. Twice—1948 and 1969.

17. 197.

18. Charles Bannerman.

19. 9—Trueman; McKenzie; Benaud; Statham; Bedser; Lindwall; Sobers; Gibbs, and Grimmett.

20. Godfrey Evans—95 minutes *v*. Australia, Adelaide, 1947.

21. Allow a fresh bowler to bowl at that end.

22. Lord Hawke—born in Lincolnshire.

23. Yes.

24. T. J. Matthews.

25. 3,816—by Denis Compton in 1947.

26. Yes.

27. Kent *v*. Worcestershire at Tunbridge Wells on June 15th, 1960.

28. 337 in 999 minutes by Hanif Mohammad, Pakistan *v*. West Indies, Bridgetown, 1958.

29. Sussex (2); Warwickshire (2); Yorkshire (2); Kent (1); Lancashire (2).

30. Call 'Dead ball', and allow the one run already run.

Appendix 2
Starting a Cricket Library

One of the joys of cricket is its literature. No other game has had such a wealth of books written about it. But quantity is less important than quality, and it is cricket's good fortune that its character has inspired the pens of those who love it. It is also a game which thrives on records, and it has created a new breed of men—the cricket statisticians, who have faithfully recorded all the facts and figures. The result is that few men can claim to have the complete cricket library though my good friend, John Arlott, must come the nearest to it. But don't be disheartened. Even he had to start, so I thought I might try to help any of you who are thinking of doing the same. It is an expensive hobby these days and some of the best books are out of print and difficult to find, in spite of the many excellent booksellers who specialize in cricket books. I have imagined that I am about to start my own library after over fifty years of reading about cricket and so the twelve books described below are essentially a personal choice. They do represent, however, a wonderful mixture of history, humour, facts, and figures and all that is best in cricket literature.

Cardus, N., *The Essential Neville Cardus*. Jonathan Cape, London, 1949 (probably the best of all the many Cardus cricket books).

Frewin, L. (ed.), *The Boundary Book*. Macdonald & Co. Ltd., London, 1962 (contributions from the famous Lord's Taverners).

Frindall, Bill, *The Kaye Book of Cricket Records*. Kaye and Ward Ltd., London, 1968 (a book containing every conceivable kind of cricket record).

Gordon, Sir Home, *That Test Match*. Duckworth, London, 1921 (a somewhat dated book with respect to its sentiments and the manner in which it is written, but one can feel the love of the game in almost every line).

Hughes, Spike, *The Art of Coarse Cricket* (new edition). Hutchinson, London, 1961 (describes in a very amusing fashion a type of cricket played by many of us, whose love of the game is greater than our ability to play it).

Macdonnell, A. G., *England Their England*. Macmillan, London, 1933. Papermac, 1967 (another humorous book with the funniest account of a match ever written).

Miller, A., *Close of Play*. St Hughe's Press Ltd., 1949 (a bedside book guaranteed to bring tears to your eyes).

Nyren, J., *The Young Cricketer's Tutor*. Gay and Bird Sportsman's Classic series, 1902 (the story of the famous Hampshire club, Hambledon).

Robertson-Glasgow, R. C., *Cricket Prints*. T. Werner-Laurie Ltd., 1943 (a fine example of the author's wit and understanding).

Ross, A. (ed.), *Cricketer's Companion*. Eyre and Spottiswoode, London, 1960 (a collection of essays, poems, cartoons, and extracts from many of the best books on cricket).

Swanton, E. W. (ed.), *The World of Cricket*. Michael Joseph Ltd., London, 1966 (a complete encyclopedia of the game).

Wisden Cricketers' Almanack (109th edition). Sporting Handbooks Ltd., London, 1972 (The Bible of cricket and the first book for any library).

Appendix 3
Glossary of Terms and Equipment

Appeals: If the fielding side believes that a batsman is out they appeal to the Umpire with the call 'How's that?' This covers every way of being out although the appealing fielders can be more specific, if they wish. Although the ball is 'dead' on 'over' being called, an appeal can still be made before the first ball of the following over is bowled, provided the bails have not been removed by both Umpires after 'Time' has been called, either for close of play or for the lunch or tea intervals.

Backing up: The non-striking batsman is said to be 'backing up' when he advances a few paces up the pitch after delivery of the ball, in expectation of a possible run. By so doing he makes it easier to 'steal' a short single. Backing up is also applied to the fielding side, when one fielder covers another in case he misses the ball. This is especially the case when the ball is returned to the wicket-keeper or bowler when the batsmen are running.

Back stroke: Usually made off a short-pitched ball. The batsman steps back with the weight on the right foot which is moved back and across in front of the stumps. It should be kept parallel to the popping crease (q.v.) while the batsman's body remains in as sideways on a position as possible.

Bails: The two bails are each $4\frac{3}{8}$ inches long and when in position in the grooves at the top of the stumps must not project more than $\frac{1}{2}$ inch above them. The stumps and bails at each end of the pitch constitute the wicket, although the pitch (q.v.) is often wrongfully called the wicket.

Ball: The ball must not weigh less than $5\frac{1}{2}$ nor more than $5\frac{3}{4}$ oz. The circumference must not be less than $8\frac{13}{16}$ inches nor more than 9 inches. It is made of red leather with an interior of cork bound with twine.

Bat: The bat must not exceed $4\frac{1}{4}$ inches in its widest part and shall not be more than 38 inches in length. There is no limit to its weight but the average bat varies from 2 lb 4 oz to 2 lb 6 oz, with some players—G. Pollock for one—using bats weighing up to 2 lb 12 oz. The blade of the bat is made of willow and the handle of cane with thin strips of rubber in between. This is bound round with twine over which is placed a rubber handle.

Batting-gloves: Worn on both hands to protect the fingers. Nowadays they are usually made of leather or cotton with a padding of stripped leather on the back of each finger and thumb. Should always be worn.

Beamer: A full pitch bowled at a batsman's head, either intentionally or unintentionally.

Block Hole: The hole made by a batsman on or just behind the popping crease, when he marks the position of his guard given by the umpire.

Bosie: The Australian name for the googly—after its inventor B. J. T. Bosanquet.

Bouncer: A short-pitched ball (*see* Bumper).

Boundary: The outside limit of the playing area. Not limited in length which is decided by the 'Home' ground authority.

Bowling crease: This crease is in line with the stumps and is 8 feet 8 inches in length with the stumps in the centre.

Box: A triangular-shaped shield made of aluminium or plastic and, like batting-gloves, should always be worn. Some boxes can be strapped round the waist but the easiest way is to wear a jock strap and place the box inside it in a specially designed pouch.

Break-back: Another name for an off-break.

Bump ball: A ball which the batsman hits hard into the ground, so that when fielded by a fielder close to the wicket it gives the appearance of being a catch.

Bumper: A short-pitched ball which rises sharply. The persistent bowling of bumpers is unfair if in the opinion of the Umpire at the bowler's end it looks like a systematic attempt at intimidation. He can then caution the bowler. If this is ineffective he must then inform the Captain of the fielding side and the other umpire. At the first repetition after this he must call 'Dead Ball', whereupon the over is considered completed and the bowler must be taken off, and cannot bowl again in that innings. No one yet has defined exactly how many bumpers constitute 'persistent'.

Bye: A run scored from a ball which passes the wicket without touching the bat or batsman and which the wicket-keeper fails to stop. If the ball touches any part of the batsman, except his hands, the runs are scored as leg-byes.

Carry one's bat: If an opening batsman is still not out when the last wicket falls he is said to have 'carried his bat'.

Championship pennant: A flag to denote the holders of the County Cricket Championship. Instituted by Warwickshire in 1951, the pennant is given by the county holding the Championship to the winners in the following season. Warwickshire gave a pennant to Surrey at the end of the 1952 season, and after winning the Championship for seven years running, they in turn gave one to Yorkshire in 1959, and so on. The pennant shows the year of the Championship, the holder's badge in the centre, and the badges of the other sixteen counties round the edge. You will always see this pennant flying over the pavilion wherever last year's Champions are playing.

Chinaman: The left-arm bowler's off-break to a right-handed batsman.

Chop: A form of late cut, made by bringing the bat *down* sharply on the ball just as it is about to pass the batsman on the off-side.

Close of play: The time arranged for play to finish. In Test matches in this country it is always 6.30 pm on the first four days and 5.30 pm (with an option of an extra half-hour at the request of either Captain) on the fifth day. In County matches on the first two days it can vary from 6.30 pm to 7.30 pm, which is the latest finishing time allowed: on the third day, play cannot be scheduled to end later than 6.30 pm or before 4.30 pm. In County cricket, if, in the opinion of both Captains 30 minutes extra at the end of the first or second day could bring about a definite result on that day, the umpires must order play to go on for half an hour after the advertised time. Once started, this 30 minutes must be completed. If the Captains disagree, the Umpires must decide. Remember that an over in progress at the advertised time for Close of Play on the *final* day of a match, must be completed at the request of either Captain, even if a wicket falls after 'time' has been reached.

Cow-shot: A swipe across the flight of a ball from off to leg which sends the ball anywhere on the leg-side.

Cross-bat: A stroke made with the bat when out of the true perpendicular; similar in principle to the 'cow-shot'.

Dead ball: The ball is 'Dead': (1) On being, in the opinion of the Umpire, finally settled in the hands of the wicket-keeper or of the bowler. (2) On reaching or pitching over the boundary. (3) On lodging in the dress of either a batsman or Umpire, whether it has been played or not. (4) On the call of 'Over' or 'Time' by the Umpire. (5) On a batsman being out for any cause. (6) In the case of unfair play or of a serious injury to a player. In addition an Umpire can also call 'Dead ball': (1) If satisfied that the striker is not ready to receive the ball. (2) If the bowler drops the ball accidentally before delivery or if the ball does not leave his hand for any reason. (3) If one or both bails fall from the striker's wicket before he receives the delivery. (4) If the batsmen attempt to steal a run during the bowler's run-up, unless the bowler throws the ball at either wicket. It should be noted that a ball does *not* become dead when it strikes an Umpire, when the wicket is broken (unless a batsman is out) or when an unsuccessful appeal is made.

Declaration of an innings: The batting Captain may declare an innings closed at any time during a match irrespective of its duration. However, in English county cricket if a match is reduced to one day owing to the weather, the batting Captain may not 'declare' until his side has batted for an hour. In county cricket a Captain can now forfeit his *second* innings instead of having to make a time-wasting declaration like 1 for 0 declared, as has happened in the past.

Donkey drop: A ball bowled very high in the air.

Draw: An undecided match. Also used to describe an old-fashioned stroke, where the batsman cocked his left leg up and deflected the ball underneath—down towards long-leg.

Drinks on the field: Drinks can only be taken to the same team in the field *once* in each session.

Duck: The dreaded score of 0.

Extras: Runs added to the score, but not actually scored by the batsman. They consist of byes, leg-byes, wides and no-balls.

Flight: The term used for a ball so delivered that in its passage through the air it deceives the batsman as to the spot where it will touch the ground. Spin aids flight as the ball is inclined to dip just before hitting the ground.

Flipper: A type of delivery which is said to have been invented by Clarrie

Grimmett and also bowled by Bruce Dooland, Richie Benaud, Bob Barber, and even by Ken Barrington. It is a ball held in the tips of the first and third fingers of the right hand. It is squeezed or flipped out of the hand from underneath the wrist—rather like flipping a cherry stone. Pitched outside the off stump it hurries through off the pitch, usually straight but sometimes from off to leg. A very useful surprise weapon if bowled occasionally, especially at a batsman who tends to play off the back foot or one who likes the pull shot off slow bowlers.

Follow-on: The side which bats first and leads by 200 runs in a match of more than four days, by 150 runs in a match of four or three days, by 100 runs in a two-day match, or by 75 runs in a one-day match, has the option of asking the other side to follow-on, i.e. to bat again immediately.

Full toss or full pitch: A ball which reaches the batsman at the popping-crease without pitching. A ball can be made into a full toss by a batsman advancing down the pitch and hitting the ball before it touches the ground.

Googly: A ball bowled out of the back of the right hand with what looks like a leg-break action, but which spins as an off-break when hitting the ground and so turns 'the wrong way', contrary to the batsman's expectations.

Go away: A ball which leaves a batsman, i.e. moves from leg to off either in the air or off the pitch, is said to 'go away'.

Go with the arm: A term for a ball which appears to go with the direction of the bowler's arm, i.e. for a right-arm bowler it is, in fact, a continuation of an out-swinger, and for a left-arm bowler, the continuation of an in-swinger, when both are bowling to a right-handed batsman.

Green wicket: A pitch well covered with plenty of grass which early in the day contains quite a lot of moisture. This is sometimes caused because the pitch has been covered all night and has 'sweated'. The greenness helps the pace bowler to get extra life and movement off the pitch.

Grub: A ball which shoots along the ground. Also called a 'sneak'.

Guard: Given to the batsman by the Umpire at the bowler's end, so that the batsman knows the position of his bat and feet in relation to the three stumps which he is guarding. Guard is given from behind the bowler's wicket unless otherwise asked for. The usual guards are: middle, middle and leg, or leg stump.

Half volley: A ball which the bat strikes just after the ball leaves the ground.

Handled ball: Either batsman may be dismissed 'handled ball' if he touches the ball, while in play, with his hands, unless he does so at the request of the fielding side.

Hat trick: The feat of a bowler taking three wickets with three consecutive deliveries either in one over or spread over two overs. By long-standing custom three wickets in three balls spread over two innings of the same match is regarded as a 'hat trick', but the limit ends there and three wickets in three balls spread over two matches do not qualify for a 'hat-trick'.

Hook: A stroke to leg off a short rising ball, pitched usually on the wicket or leg-side.

In-swinger: A ball which swings from off to leg in flight, thus moving into the batsman while still in the air.

King pair: If a batsman is out first ball for 0 in each innings, he is said to have made a 'king pair'.

Lap: An expression used by modern cricketers to describe a cross-bat stroke. The batsman hits across the flight of the ball and even though it pitches on or outside the off stump, he hits it somewhere between square-leg and mid-on.

Last over: The over in progress at the close of play on the final day of the match shall be completed at the request of either Captain, even if a wicket falls after 'Time' has been called. The last over before close of play or an interval shall be started provided that the Umpire standing at square-leg, after walking at his normal pace, has arrived at his position behind the stumps at the bowler's end before time has been reached. This rule will also apply if a batsman is out or 'retires' after the last ball of an over when less than two minutes remain for play at the end of the match.

Late cut: A stroke played to a short ball outside the off stump by stepping across with the right foot and hitting the ball down with a wristy action, so sending it past the slips.

Leg-break: A ball which turns on the pitch from the leg-side to the off. The orthodox spin for a left arm bowler is a leg-break to a right-handed batsman.

Leg-byes: Leg-byes are scored when the ball is *unintentionally* deflected by the batsman with any part of his person except the hand or hands holding the bat *when he is attempting to play the ball*. Deliberate deflection is unfair and as soon as the Umpire is satisfied that the fielding side has no chance of dismissing either batsmen, he must call Dead Ball. Any runs which have been scored are then cancelled. In deciding whether a deflection is deliberate the criterion shall be whether or not *the batsman has attempted to play the ball with the bat*.

Leg-cutter: A fast leg-break which is bowled by 'cutting' across the seam of the ball rather than using the normal wrist-spin.

Leg-side: The side of the pitch *behind* the batsman as he takes his stand at the wicket. The number of fielders on the leg-side *behind the popping crease* must not exceed two at the instant of the bowler's delivery. If there are more than two the square-leg Umpire must call 'No-ball'.

Leg-trap: A term used to describe a cluster of fielders in the short-leg positions.

Length: A good-length ball is one which pitches on the pitch at such a distance from the batsman as to make him uncertain whether to play a backward or forward stroke. It is a ball which he cannot reach comfortably by playing forward, or adequately deal with by playing back, as the ball is too far up for the latter type of stroke.

Lob: A method of bowling which is rarely seen in first-class cricket today. Bowled under-arm, it is a survivor of the earliest known form of bowling. If the ball is returned under-arm by the fielder he is said to 'lob' it.

Long field: The part of the outfield in front of the sight-screen in the region of long-off and long-on.

Long handle: The aggressive batsman who is hitting out is sometimes said to be 'using the long handle'.

Long hop: A very short-pitched ball.

Maiden over: An over off which no runs are scored by the batsmen.

Middle: The centre of the ground or the square upon which the pitches are prepared.

New ball: Either Captain can demand a new ball at the start of each innings. The Captain of the fielding side has the option of taking another new ball after 85 overs have been bowled with the old one. The taking of the new ball can be delayed but the counting of overs for another ball does not start until this new ball has been taken (i.e. if a Captain delays taking a new ball until 100 overs have been bowled, the next new ball is due after 185th over). In Australia and New Zealand the new ball can be taken after 65 of the standard eight-ball overs.

Night-watchman: A lower-order batsman sent in to play out time when a wicket falls shortly before close of play. This saves the risk of a better batsman losing his wicket—often in failing light.

No-ball: For a delivery to be fair, the ball must be bowled not thrown. If either Umpire be not entirely satisfied of the absolute fairness of a delivery in this respect, he shall call and signal 'No-ball' instantly upon delivery. The Umpire at the bowler's wicket shall call and signal 'No-ball' if, in the delivery stride no part of the bowler's front foot is behind the popping crease, whether grounded or raised, or if he is not satisfied that the bowler's back foot has landed within (but not touching) the return crease or its forward extension.

A ball shall be deemed to have been thrown if, in the opinion of either Umpire the process of straightening the bowling arm, whether it be partial or complete, takes place during that part of the delivery swing which directly precedes the ball leaving the hand. This definition shall not debar a bowler *from straightening an over-extended arm* nor from the use of the wrist in the delivery swing.

In conjunction with the above-mentioned experimental law the following conditions shall apply: (1) The length of the return crease shall be 4 feet. (2) The popping crease shall extend 6 feet either side of the line of stumps. (3) The popping crease and return crease shall be re-drawn during each interval.

The Umpire will also call 'No ball': (1) If the bowler fails to notify the batsman that he is changing his delivery, i.e. from over the wicket to round the wicket, from over-arm to lobs, etc. (2) If there are more than two fielders behind the popping crease on the leg-side. (3) If a bowler, before delivery, throws the ball at the striker's wicket even in an attempt to run him out.

The following points are also important: (1) A batsman may be out in four ways off 'No-ball': Run out, handling the ball, obstructing the field, hitting the ball twice. (2) The ball does *not* become dead upon the call of 'No ball', and if runs are scored by the batsman they are credited to the score and debited to the bowler. If no runs are scored, then one 'No ball' is added to the extras. (3) Any byes or leg-byes made off a 'No ball' are scored as 'No balls'. (4) A 'No ball' does *not* count in the over so an extra ball has to be bowled for every 'No ball' bowled, in order that the 'Over' may consist of six legitimate deliveries. (5) The Umpire signals 'No-ball' by extending one arm horizontally.

Off-break: A ball which after pitching turns from off to leg. Bowled by a right-arm bowler, it is referred to as orthodox spin. Spun mainly by the first finger of the right hand, the action is like turning a door handle.

Off-cutter: A fast off-break bowled by 'cutting' across the seam of the ball rather than by orthodox finger spin.

Off-drive: A drive made off the front foot, usually from a half-volley, in the arc between cover-point and long-off.

Off side: The side of the field 'in front' of the batsman as he takes his stand at the wicket.

On-drive: A drive made off the front foot in the arc between mid-wicket and long-on.

On side: The same as the leg side, i.e. the side of the field behind the batsman.

Outfield: That portion of the playing area which is some distance from the pitch. The fielding positions are nearer the boundary than the pitch (e.g. long-off, long-on, deep third man, long-leg, deep mid-wicket, etc.).

Over: An 'Over' of six balls is bowled from each end alternately. For first-class cricket in Australia and New Zealand the eight-ball 'Over' is in force.

Out of his ground: The batsman must have some part of his bat or his foot on the ground behind the popping crease in order to avoid being run out or stumped. If he does not he is held to be 'Out of his ground'. The foot positioned on the line is 'Out'. It is not enough for a batsman to have a foot or the bat in the air behind the crease, *it must be grounded*.

Out-swinger: A ball which swings from leg to off in flight, often described as 'leaving the bat'.

Over the wicket: A term used to describe from which side of the stumps a bowler is bowling. A right-arm bowler delivers the ball from the left hand-side, a left-arm bowler from the right.

Overthrow: A throw in from the field which eludes the wicket-keeper or bowler and travels beyond the stumps to the other side of the field, so that the batsmen may take further runs. If a ball hits the stumps with a batsman in his crease, and then ricochets off to the outfield, overthrows may still be taken even though the wicket is broken. All such runs scored are credited to the striker and (rather bad luck this) debited to the bowler, unless of course they are extras to start with.

Pair of spectacles: A term used to describe the performance of a batsman who fails to score in both innings of a match, thereby collecting two 'ducks'.

Payment of players and umpires in Test matches:

Players	£150 per match
Twelfth man on duty throughout	£65
Twelfth man (first and second day)	£40
Twelfth man (third, fourth, and fifth day)	£25
Umpires	£100 per match
Scorers	£25 per match
Emergency fielders	£5 per day

Pitch: A playing area 22 yards long and 5 feet in width on either side of a line joining the two middle stumps. A pitch may not be changed *during* a match unless it becomes unfit for play, and then only with the consent of *both* Captains.

Played on: A colloquial term used for a batsman who is dismissed 'Bowled' through hitting the ball into his own wicket with the bat.

Playing back: A stroke played by the batsman with his weight on the back foot, i.e. the foot nearest the stumps and the right foot in the case of a right-handed batsman. This stroke is usually used when playing a ball which is short of a length.

Plumb pitch or wicket: A perfect surface which has not been affected by either rain or wear. It gives no help to swing or spin bowlers as the ball comes off at a uniform height and pace, without any real change of direction. Ideal for batting.

Polishing the ball: (1) No one, other than the bowler, may polish the ball. (2) No one (including the bowler) may rub the ball on the pitch or ground or interfere in any way with the natural condition of the ball. Wiping and cleaning is allowed under the Umpire's supervision.

Pop: A ball which lifts sharply off the pitch is said to 'Pop'.

Popping crease: A line 4 feet in front of the wicket parallel to the bowling crease. It is the forward limit of the batsman's safety area against stumping and run-out decisions.

Pull: A stroke made by hitting across the flight of a ball delivered on the stumps or off-side of the wicket and driving it away to the on-side. This is technically a forward stroke off the front foot. The bat remains perpendicular throughout as distinct from the cow-shot.

Registration and qualification rules: These are rather complicated but in simple terms are as follows:
1. *Home-born players:* Can play (*a*) For the county of his birth. (*b*) For the county in which he has lived for the previous twelve consecutive months. (*c*) For the county for which he is specially registered (a county can apply for special registration for up to two cricketers in any one calendar year and must give a contract for a minimum of three years). If a cricketer wants to leave his county to play for another against the wishes of his county, then he can only qualify for the other county by living in it for up to a maximum of twelve consecutive months, the exact period to be decided by the Registration Committee.
2. *Overseas-born player:* Each county may register one overseas-born player immediately without any qualification period being required. But they can only have two registered overseas players on their books at any one time, and can only make another immediate registration of another overseas player after three years. Once an overseas player has been immediately registered by a county he can *never* be so registered again. If he wishes to play for another county he must qualify by a twelve month residence. An overseas-born player becomes a home-born player when he has lived in this country for ten years, and when playing for a county he must be made available to play in Test Matches for the country of his birth, either here in England, or in his own country.

Retirements: A batsman may retire at any time but cannot resume his innings without the consent of the fielding Captain and then only *at the fall of a wicket.* A batsman is regarded as 'Not out' if he retires as a result of injury or illness but it counts as 'Out' if he retires for any other reason.

Return crease: A line which turns back at right angles at each end of the bowling crease and is deemed to be of unlimited length. Since the introduction of the front foot law for calling 'No-balls', the return crease is extended from the bowling crease to the popping crease.

Rolling, mowing, and watering: The pitch cannot be rolled during a match except before the start of each innings and of each day's play, when, if the Captain of the batting side chooses, it can be swept and rolled for *not more than 7 minutes.* It can be rolled for less if the Captain so wishes. Rolling before play must take place not *more* than 30 minutes before play is due to start, and the Captain of the batting side can delay this rolling until ten minutes before the start if he wishes. But if the Captain of the batting side only declares his innings closed just before the start, the time for sufficient rolling must be taken out of the normal playing period, if necessary. This also applies if a declaration is made later than 15 minutes after the start of the lunch interval. Play will then not restart until 2.20 pm. (2) The pitch will be mown under the supervision of the umpires before play begins on alternate days after the start of a match. This means that in a Test Match in this country starting on a Thursday the pitch *can* be mown before the start and then *must* be mown on the Saturday and Monday. (Sunday counting as a playing day.) If owing to rain the pitch is not mown on the appointed day, it must be mown on the first day on which play is resumed and then on alternate days for the rest of the match. In first-class matches of three days the pitch must be mown on the third day. In week-end matches Sunday counts as a day so that the pitch must be mown on Monday. If conditions permit the outfield will be mown before the start of play on each morning of the match. The pitch *cannot* be watered in any circumstances during a match.

Round the wicket: To bowl round the wicket a right-arm bowler delivers the ball from the right-hand side of the stumps, and a left-arm bowler from the left-hand side.

Run-up: To cut out time-wasting the bowler is not now allowed a trial run-up after 'Play' has been called in any session, except at the fall of a wicket and then only if it will not cause any waste of time.

Seam bowler or seamer: A bowler—normally of medium pace or faster—who 'moves' the ball in the air or off the pitch.

Session: A session is one of the three official periods of play, i.e. from start to lunch, from lunch to tea, from tea to close of play.

Set: A batsman is said to be 'Set' when he has got his 'eye in' or has 'played himself in'.

Shine: 'Shine on the ball' means that it still retains some of the smooth polished surface which it had when new. A smooth surface helps the ball to swing, which is why you see seam bowlers polishing the ball (q.v.).

Shooter: A ball which does not rise after hitting the ground. Also referred to as a 'squatter'.

Short run: When a batsman fails to make good his ground at one end when running two or more runs. The umpire signals this, and the scorers delete one or more runs from those actually run by the batsmen.

Shoulder arms: An expression used to describe a batsman's action when he holds the bat aloft over his shoulder as he allows the ball to go by on the off-side without attempting a stroke.

Sight-screen: In Test Matches in this country sight-screens must now be provided at both ends of the ground.

Square cut: A stroke made to a short ball outside the off stump by stepping across the wicket and hitting the ball down with a wristy action as it is level with the batsman. This stroke will normally send the ball between Cover Point and Gully down towards Third Man.

Start of play: In Test Matches in this country it is always at 11.30 am on the first four days and at 11 am on the fifth day.

In other first-class matches it varies but can never be *before* 11 am. Normally it is either 11.30 am or 12 noon, except in September when some matches start at 11 am even on the first day.

Stumps: Must be of equal size and placed into the ground so that the ball cannot pass between them. When in position the three stumps together are 9 inches wide, each stump being 28 inches above the ground.

Substitutes: A substitute is allowed to field or act as a runner for any player who may be incapacitated by illness or injury *during the match* but not for any other reason.

The consent of the opposing Captain always has to be obtained for a person to act as substitute, and he may also indicate positions in which the substitute may *not* field. A substitute may not bat or bowl. It is also generally accepted that a substitute may not keep wicket, but there is nothing in the rules to stop him from doing so, provided the opposing Captain has not indicated it as one of the positions he may not field in.

Under the laws a substitute is allowed only as a result of injury to another player *sustained in the match.* If a player starts the match injured and then finds himself unable to carry on, the opposing Captain has the perfect right to refuse a substitute. A player may subsequently bat, bowl or field, even though a substitute has acted for him earlier in the match.

When he is the striker a player with a substitute who is running for him can be out 'Stumped' or 'Run out' at the wicket-keeper's end. When not the striker the injured batsman is considered out of the game and stands out of the way near the square-leg Umpire.

Sweep: A stroke played with a horizontal bat at a ball which is usually on or outside the leg stump. The bat follows round and hits the ball behind the wicket on the leg-side, down towards long leg or fine leg.

Tail: The players engaged more for their bowling or wicket-keeping abilities than for their prowess as batsmen and who are not expected to score many runs are known as the 'Tail' or 'Tail-enders'. They are also sometimes referred to as 'Rabbits'. One player was so notoriously bad as a batsman that he gained the nickname of 'Ferret'—the man who comes in after the 'Rabbits'.

Tea interval: The regulations governing this are the nightmare of commentators, spectators and even Umpires! Basically they are as given on page 36.

Team: A first-class match is played between two teams of eleven players each. Before tossing for choice of innings the two Captains must exchange lists of their teams *in writing*, together with the twelfth man. Afterwards no alteration can be made in either team without the consent of the opposing Captain. In practice this will probably be given in the event of sudden illness or injury *before the match starts*.

Tie: A match which ends with an equal total of runs scored by each side, provided that the fourth innings is completed.

Top spin: Spin which allows the ball to gain pace off the pitch when hitting the ground and then to continue on the same line. Bowled by leg-break bowlers in addition to the googly.

Toss for innings: The choice of innings is decided by the toss of a coin. The home Captain tosses the coin and the away Captain calls. The toss must be made not less than 15 minutes before the time for start of play, and is, in fact, usually made at 11 am for a match due to start at 11.30 am. If, owing to inclement weather, no start seems possible, the toss can be delayed until such time as the game can be started. But if the toss is made and rain then holds up the start of the match, the toss stands and the decision of the Captain holds.

Track: A slang expression for the pitch. A batsman is sometimes said to 'go down the track' to a slow bowler.

Umpires: Two Umpires are appointed and cannot be changed during a match without the consent of *both* Captains. Before the toss for innings they must agree with the Captains any special regulations and all conditions affecting the match, i.e. hours of play, intervals, which clock they are going by, choice of balls to be used, and any local rule affecting the boundary.

They must also see that the wickets are properly pitched and that all playing equipment such as bats, balls, and stumps conform to the laws. As shown elsewhere, in addition to interpreting the laws, the Umpires have special powers to stop a bowler from bowling any more in an innings, if (1) he is guilty of bowling persistent bumpers. (2) If he causes damage to the pitch in his follow through. (The 'danger area' is an area contained by an imaginary line 4 feet from and parallel to the popping-crease and within two imaginary and parallel lines drawn down the pitch from points 1 foot on either side of the middle stump.) (3) If he takes unnecessarily long to bowl an over.

In each of the above cases the Umpire must warn the bowler the first time, the next time the Captain and other Umpire, and on the third occasion call 'Dead ball'.

An Umpire may alter his decision provided that he does it promptly. He must also intervene if a batsman, not having been given out, has left his wicket under a misapprehension.

The various Umpires' signals are shown on pages 152–53.

Wasting time: Umpires are reminded that any waste of time—such as a bowler wasting time, the fielders crossing over slowly between 'Overs' or for left-handed batsmen, fielders throwing the ball to one another before returning it to the bowler (unless the bowler begins his walk back to his mark immediately after delivering the ball), Captains being unduly deliberate in field placing and not starting such field placing until a new batsman has reached the wicket, incoming batsmen taking too long to reach the wicket constitutes unfair play, and after consultation together and, where possible, after warning the Captain concerned, they shall report such occurrences to the Secretary of MCC and to the Manager or Secretary of the team giving offence.

Byes: by raising the open hand above the head.
Leg-byes: by touching a raised knee with the hand.

No-balls: by extending one arm horizontally.
Out: by raising the index finger above the head.

In the event of a bowler taking unnecessarily long to bowl an over, the Umpire at the bowler's end, after consultation with the other Umpire, shall take the following immediate action: (1) Caution the bowler and inform the Captain of the fielding side that he has done so. (2) Should this caution prove ineffective, direct the Captain of the fielding side to take the bowler off at the end of the over in progress, report the occurrence to the Captain of the batting side as soon as an interval of play takes place, send a written report of the occurrence to the Secretary of MCC and to the Manager or Secretary of the team to which the

One short: by raising the arm upwards and by touching the shoulder nearest to the scorers with the tips of the fingers.
Wides: by extending both arms horizontally.

Six: by raising both hands above the head.
Boundaries: by waving the hand from side to side.

offending player belongs. A bowler who has been 'taken off' as above may not bowl again during the same innings.

Wicket-keeper: A wicket-keeper must not have any part of his person in front of the wicket until the ball delivered by the bowler touches the bat or person of the batsman or passes the wicket, or until the batsman attempts a run. Otherwise the batsman *may* be given 'Not out', 'Bowled', 'Caught', 'Stumped', or LBW. But if in the opinion of the umpire the encroachment by the wicket-keeper has not gained any advantage for the fielding side, nor in any way interferred with the right of the striker to play the ball with complete freedom, nor has had any effect whatsoever in the downfall of the striker, then the Umpire shall disregard the infringement.

Wicket maiden: An over off which no runs are scored by the batsman but in which the bowler takes one or more wickets.

Wide ball: The ball is called 'Wide' if it is bowled so high over or so wide of the wicket that in the Umpire's opinion the ball is out of the reach of a batsman when taking guard *in the normal position.*

Wisden trophy: A trophy which is played for by England and the West Indies. Presented by Wisden to celebrate their centenary.

Wrong-un: Another term used to denote the googly, called a 'Bosie' in Australia after B. J. T. Bosanquet, the originator.

Yorker: A ball well pitched up so that it touches the ground at the batsman's feet and is liable to pass under the bat. A very useful ball for a pace bowler to bowl at a new batsman.

Appendix 4
Main Cricket Records

All records are complete to the end of the 1971 English season. The Test records include the unofficial Tests played by South Africa since she forfeited membership of the ICC in 1961, and the unofficial Tests between England and the Rest of the World played in 1970.

* denotes a not-out innings or an unfinished partnership.

A. ALL FIRST-CLASS CRICKET
1. Team Records
Highest Innings Total
   1,107   Victoria v. New South Wales (Melbourne) 1926–27
Highest Second Innings Total
   770   New South Wales v. South Australia (Adelaide) 1920–21
Highest Fourth Innings Total
   654 for 5 (set 696)   England v. South Africa (Durban)..............1938–39
Highest Match Aggregate
   2,376 (for 38 wkts)   Bombay v. Maharashtra (Poona) 1948–49
Largest Margin of Victory
   Innings and 851 runs: Railways v. Dera Ismail Khan (Lahore) 1964–65
Most Runs in a Day
   721   Australians v. Essex (Southend) 1948
Lowest Innings Total
   12   Oxford University v. MCC (Oxford) 1877
   12   Northamptonshire v. Gloucestershire (Gloucester)..............1907
Lowest Match Aggregate by One Team
   34   Border (16 and 18) v. Natal (East London) 1959–60
Lowest Match Aggregate—Both Teams in Completed Match
   105 (for 31 wkts)   MCC v. Australians (Lord's) 1878
Fewest Runs in a Day
   95   Australia (80) v. Pakistan (15 for 2) at Karachi 1956–57
Team Scoring Most Centuries in an Innings
   6   Holkar (912 for 8 dec.) v. Mysore (Indore) 1945–46

2. Players' Records (Individual Batting)
Highest Individual Innings
   499   Hanif Mohammad: Karachi v. Bahawalpur (Karachi) 1958–59
Most Hundreds in Successive Innings
   6   C. B. Fry for Sussex and Rest of England 1901
   6   D. G. Bradman for South Australia and Bradman's XI 1938–39
   6   M. J. Procter for Rhodesia 1970–71
Most Hundreds in a Season
   18   D. C. S. Compton for England, Middlesex and The South 1947

Two Double-Centuries in a Match
  A. E. Fagg (244 and 202*)   Kent *v.* Essex (Colchester) 1938
Most Hundreds in a Career
  197   J. B. Hobbs (Surrey) 1905–34
Highest Score on Debut
  240   W. F. E. Marx: Transvaal *v.* Griqualand West (Johannesburg) 1920–21
Hundreds in First Three Innings in First-class Cricket
  J. S. Solomon (114*, 108, 121) for British Guiana in 1956–57 and 1957–58
Most Runs in a Season
  3,816 (Avge 90·85): D. C. S. Compton (Middlesex) 1947
Thousand Runs in a Season Most Times
  28   W. G. Grace (Gloucestershire) and F. E. Woolley (Kent)
Earliest Dates for Scoring 1,000, 2,000 and 3,000 Runs in a Season
  1,000 runs: May 27th (1938)—D. G. Bradman (Australians)
  2,000 runs: July 5th (1906)—T. W. Hayward (Surrey)
  3,000 runs: August 20th (1906)—T. W. Hayward (Surrey)
               August 20th (1937)—W. R. Hammond (Gloucestershire)
Most Runs in a Career
  61,237 (Avge 50·65): J. B. Hobbs (Surrey) 1905–34
Carrying Bat Through *both* Innings of a Match
  H. Jupp 43* 109*   Surrey *v.* Yorkshire (Oval) 1874
  S. P. Kinneir 70* 69*   Warwickshire *v.* Leicestershire (Leicester) 1907
  C. J. B. Wood 107* 117*   Leicestershire *v.* Yorkshire (Bradford) 1911
  V. M. Merchant 135* 77*   Indians *v.* Lancashire (Liverpool) 1936
Fast Scoring
  Fastest 50: 8 min   C. Inman: Leicestershire *v.* Nottinghamshire
    (Nottingham) 1965
  Fastest 100: 35 min   P. G. H. Fender: Surrey *v.* Northamp-
    tonshire (Northampton) 1920
  Fastest 200: 120 min   G. L. Jessop: Gloucestershire *v.* Sussex
    (Hove) 1903
  Fastest 300: 181 min   D. C. S. Compton: MCC *v.* North-Eastern
    Transvaal (Benoni) 1948–49
Most Runs in a Day
  345   C. G. Macartney: Australians *v.* Nottinghamshire (Nottingham) 1921
Most Runs Off One Over
  36   (666666) G. St. A. Sobers off M. A. Nash: Nottinghamshire
    v. Glamorgan (Swansea) 1968
Most Sixes in an Innings
  15   J. R. Reid: Wellington *v.* Northern Districts (Wellington) 1962–63
Most Sixes in a Match
  17   W. J. Stewart: Warwickshire *v.* Lancashire (Blackpool) 1959
Most Sixes in a Season
  72   A. W. Wellard (Somerset)..1935
Most Boundaries in an Innings
  68   (all fours) P. A. Perrin: Essex *v.* Derbyshire (Chesterfield) 1904
Slow Scoring
  Slowest 50: 361 min   T. E. Bailey: England *v.* Australia (Brisbane) 1958–59

Slowest 100: 545 min   D. J. McGlew: South Africa *v.* Australia
(Durban) 1957–58
Slowest 200: 570 min   S. G. Barnes: Australia *v.* England (Sydney) 1946–47
Longest Time Before Scoring First Run
95 min   T. G. Evans (10*): England *v.* Australia (Adelaide).........1946–47
Longest Individual Innings
999 min   Hanif Mohammad (337): Pakistan *v.* West Indies
(Bridgetown) 1957–58
Lowest Innings Totals to Include Individual Milestones
A Fifty: 66   Indians *v.* Yorkshire (Harrogate) 1932   ....S. Nazir Ali 52
A Century: 144   Kent *v.* Warwickshire (Folkestone) 1931   F. E. Woolley 103*
A Double-century: 298   Gloucestershire *v.* Glamorgan (Newport) 1956
T. W. Graveney 200
A Triple-century: 387   Rest *v.* Hindus (Bombay) 1943–44 Vijay Hazare 309
A Quadruple-century: 793   Victoria *v.* Queensland (Melbourne) 1927–28
W. H. Ponsford 437

3. Players' Records (Batting Partnerships)
World Record for Each Wicket
1st 555   P. Holmes and H. Sutcliffe: Yorkshire *v.* Essex (Leyton)...1932
2nd 455   K. V. Bhandarkar and B. B. Nimbalkar: Maharashtra *v.*
Kathiawar (Poona) 1948–49
3rd 445   P. E. Whitelaw and W. N. Carson: Auckland *v.* Otago
(Dunedin)...1936–37
4th 577   Gul Mahomed and Vijay Hazare: Baroda *v.* Holkar
(Baroda) 1946–47
5th 405   S. G. Barnes and D. G. Bradman: Australia *v.* England (Sydney) 1946–47
6th 487*   G. A. Headley and C. C. Passailaigue: Jamaica *v.*
Tennyson's XI (Kingston)...1931–32
7th 347   D. St. E. Atkinson and C. C. Depeiza: West Indies *v.*
Australia (Bridgetown) 1954–55
8th 433   V. T. Trumper and A. Sims: Australians *v.* Canterbury (Christchurch) 1913–14
9th 283   A. R. Warren and J. Chapman: Derbyshire *v.* Warwickshire (Blackwell) 1910
10th 307   A. F. Kippax and J. E. H. Hooker: New South Wales
v. Victoria (Melbourne)..1928–29

4. Players' Records (Bowling)
All Ten Wickets in an Innings at Least Cost
10 for 10   H. Verity: Yorkshire *v.* Nottinghamshire (Leeds).........1932
All Ten Wickets in an Innings on Most Occasions
3   A. P. Freeman:
10 for 131   Kent *v.* Lancashire (Maidstone) 1929
10 for 53   Kent *v.* Essex (Southend) 1930
10 for 79   Kent *v.* Lancashire (Manchester)..................1931

Most Wickets in a Match
  19   J. C. Laker (9 for 37 and 10 for 53): England *v.* Australia
       (Manchester) 1956
Most Wickets in a Day
  17   C. Blythe: Kent *v.* Northamptonshire (Northampton)...........1907
  17   H. Verity: Yorkshire *v.* Essex (Leyton) 1933
  17   T. W. Goddard: Gloucestershire *v.* Kent (Bristol) 1939
Most Wickets in a Season
  304 (Avge 18·05) A. P. Freeman (Kent) 1928
Hundred Wickets in a Season Most Times
  23   W. Rhodes (Yorkshire)
Earliest Dates for Taking 100, 200, and 300 Wickets in a Season
  100 wickets: June 12th (1896)—J. T. Hearne (Middlesex)
               June 12th (1931)—C. W. L. Parker (Gloucestershire)
  200 wickets: July 27th (1928)—A. P. Freeman (Kent)
  300 wickets: September 15th (1928)—A. P. Freeman (Kent)
Most Wickets in a Career
  4,187 (Avge 16·71) W. Rhodes (Yorkshire) 1898–1930
Four Wickets with Consecutive Balls (since 1946)
  F. Ridgway: Kent *v.* Derbyshire (Folkestone) 1951
  A. K. Walker: Nottinghamshire *v.* Leicestershire (Leicester) 1956
  S. N. Mohol: Combined XI *v.* President's XI (Poona) 1965–66
Most Hat-tricks in a Career
  7   D. V. P. Wright (Kent)
Performing Hat-trick Twice in Same Innings
  A. E. Trott: Middlesex *v.* Somerset (Lord's) 1907
  J. S. Rao: Services *v.* Northern Punjab (Amritsar) 1963–64
Most Runs Conceded in an Innings
  362 A. A. Mailey (64-0–362-4): NSW *v.* Victoria (Mel-
       bourne) 1926–27
Most Runs Conceded in a Match
  428 C. S. Nayudu (6 for 153 and 5 for 275): Holkar *v.* Bombay
       (Bombay)..1944–45
Most Balls Bowled in an Innings
  588 S. Ramadhin (98-35–179-2): West Indies ˙ *v.* England
       (Birmingham) 1957
Most Balls Bowled in a Match
  917 C. S. Nayudu (152·5-25–428-11): Holkar *v.* Bom-
       bay (Bombay) 1944–45
Bowlers Unchanged Through Both Completed Innings of a Match (Since 1946)
  D. Shackleton and V. H. D. Cannings: Hampshire *v.* Kent
       (Southampton) 1952
  D. Shackleton and M. Heath: Hampshire *v.* Derbyshire (Burton-
       upon-Trent) 1958
  Rajinder Pal and P. Sitaram: Delhi *v.* Jammu and Kashmir
       (Srinagar)..1960–61
  B. S. Crump and R. R. Bailey: Northamptonshire *v.* Glamorgan
       (Cardiff) 1967

Most Maiden Overs in Succession
  6-ball overs: 21   R. G. Nadkarni—India *v.* England (Madras) 1963–64
  8-ball overs: 16 H. J. Tayfield—South Africa *v.* England (Durban)
  1956–57

5. Players' Records (All-round Cricket)

Outstanding 'Doubles'
  2,000 runs and 200 wickets: G. H. Hirst (Yorkshire) in 1906
  3,000 runs and 100 wickets: J. H. Parks (Sussex) in 1937
  1,000 runs and 200 wickets: A. E. Trott (Middlesex) in 1899 and 1900
                                       A. S. Kennedy (Hampshire) in 1922
                                       M. W. Tate (Sussex) in 1923, 1924, and 1925
Most 'Doubles'
  16 W. Rhodes (Yorkshire)
Fastest 'Double'
  June 28th (1906) G. H. Hirst (Yorkshire) in only sixteen matches
Outstanding Match Doubles—Century and Ten Wickets in an Innings
  V. E. Walker (108 and 10 for 74): England XI *v.* Surrey (Oval) 1859
  E. M. Grace (192* and 10 for 69): MCC *v.* Gentleman of Kent
    (Canterbury) 1862
  W. G. Grace (104 and 10 for 49): MCC *v.* Oxford U. (Oxford) 1886

6. Players' Records (Fielding)

Most Catches in an Innings
  7 M. J. Stewart: Surrey *v.* Northamptonshire (Northampton) 1957
  7 A. S. Brown: Gloucestershire *v.* Nottinghamshire (Nottingham) 1966
Most Catches in a Match
  10 W. R. Hammond: Gloucestershire *v.* Surrey (Cheltenham)...... 1928
Most Catches in a Season
  78 W. R. Hammond (Gloucestershire) 1928
Most Catches in a Career
  1,011 F. E. Woolley (Kent) 1906–38

7. Players' Records (Wicket-keeping)

Most Dismissals and Catches in an Innings
  8 (8 ct) A. T. W. Grout: Queensland *v.* Western Australia (Bris-
    bane) 1959–60
Most Stumpings in an Innings
  6 H. Yarnold: Worcestershire *v.* Scotland (Dundee) 1951
Most Dismissals in a Match
  12 (8 ct, 4 st) E. Pooley: Surrey *v.* Sussex (Oval).................... 1868
  12 (9 ct, 3 st) D. Tallon: Queensland *v.* NSW (Sydney) 1938–39
  12 (9 ct, 3 st) H. B. Taber: NSW *v.* South Australia (Adelaide) ...1968–69
Most Catches in a Match
  11 A. Long: Surrey *v.* Sussex (Hove) 1964

Most Stumpings in a Match
  9   F. H. Huish: Kent *v.* Surrey (Oval) 1911
Most Dismissals in a Season
  127   L. E. G. Ames (Kent)—79 ct, 48 st.............................1929
Most Catches in a Season
  96   J. G. Binks (Yorkshire)..1960
Most Stumpings in a Season
  64   L. E. G. Ames (Kent) 1932
Wicket-keepers' 'Double' of 1,000 Runs and 100 Dismissals in a Season
  L. E. G. Ames (Kent) in 1928, 1929, and 1932
  J. T. Murray (Middlesex) in 1957
Most Dismissals and Catches in a Career
  1,493   (1,235 ct, 258 st) H. Strudwick (Surrey) 1902–27
Most Stumpings in a Career
  415   L. E. G. Ames (Kent) 1926–51
Largest Innings Without Byes
  672 for 7 d   A. P. Wickham: Somerset *v.* Hampshire (Taunton) ...1899

B. TEST CRICKET ONLY

Key to abbreviations used

E	England	A	Australia
SA	South Africa	WI	West Indies
NZ	New Zealand	I	India
P	Pakistan	RW	Rest of the World

1. Results Summary

Test Matches—1876–77 to 1971 inclusive

		Tests	*E*	*A*	*SA*	*WI*	*NZ*	*I*	*P*	*RW*	*Tied*	*Dr*
England	*v.* Australia	209	68	80	—	—	—	—	—	—	—	61
	v. South Africa	102	46	—	18	—	—	—	—	—	—	38
	v. West Indies	58	20	—	—	16	—	—	—	—	—	22
	v. New Zealand	42	20	—	—	—	0	—	—	—	—	22
	v. India	40	18	—	—	—	—	4	—	—	—	18
	v. Pakistan	21	9	—	—	—	—	—	1	—	—	11
	v. Rest of World	5	1	—	—	—	—	—	—	4	—	0
Australia	*v.* South Africa	53	—	29	11	—	—	—	—	—	—	13
	v. West Indies	30	—	17	—	6	—	—	—	—	1	6
	v. New Zealand	1	—	1	—	—	0	—	—	—	—	0
	v. India	25	—	16	—	—	—	3	—	—	—	6
	v. Pakistan	6	—	2	—	—	—	—	1	—	—	3

South Africa v. New Zealand	17	—	—	9	—	2	—	—	—	—	6
West Indies v. New Zealand	9	—	—	—	5	2	—	—	—	—	2
v. India	28	—	—	—	12	—	1	—	—	—	15
v. Pakistan	8	—	—	—	4	—	—	3	—	—	1
New Zealand v. India	16	—	—	—	—	2	7	—	—	—	7
v. Pakistan	12	—	—	—	—	1	—	4	—	—	7
India v. Pakistan	15	—	—	—	—	—	2	1	—	—	12
	697	182	145	38	43	7	17	10	4	1	250

	Tests	Won	Lost	Drawn	Tied	Toss won
England	477	182	123	172	—	240
Australia	324	145	89	89	1	155
South Africa	172	38	77	57	—	80
West Indies	133	43	43	46	1	74
New Zealand	97	7	46	44	—	54
India	124	17	49	58	—	59
Pakistan	62	10	18	34	—	33
Rest of World	5	4	1	—	—	2

2. Team Records

Highest Innings Total
    903 for 7 d   England v. Australia (Oval) 1938
Highest Fourth Innings Totals
    To Win: 404 for 3   Australia v. England (Leeds) 1948
    To Draw: 654 for 5   England v. South Africa (Durban) 1938–39
    To Lose: 411   England v. Australia (Sydney) 1924–25
Highest Match Aggregate
    1,981 (for 35 wkts)   South Africa v. England (Durban) 1938–39
Lowest Innings Total
    26   New Zealand v. England (Auckland) 1954–55
Lowest Match Aggregate (Completed Match)
    234 (for 29 wkts)   Australia v. South Africa (Melbourne)............1931–32
Largest Margin of Victory
    Innings and 579 runs: England v. Australia (Oval).....................1938
The Only Test Tie
    Australia v. West Indies (Brisbane) 1960–61
Longest Match
    10 days: South Africa v. England (Durban) 1938–39
Side Dismissed Twice in a Day
    England (65 and 72) v. Australia (Sydney) on third day 1894–95
    India (58 and 82) v. England at Manchester on third day 1952

Most Runs in One Day
One Team: 503 (for 2 wkts)   England *v.* South Africa (Lord's) 1924
Both Teams: 588 (for 6 wkts)   England (398 for 6) *v.* India
(190 for 0) (Manchester) 1936
Least Runs in a Full Day's Play
95   Australia (80) *v.* Pakistan (15 for 2) (Karachi) 1956–57
Most Hundreds in an Innings
5   Australia *v.* West Indies (Kingston) 1954–55

3. Players' Records (Individual Batting)

Highest Individual Innings
365 *   G. St. A. Sobers: West Indies *v.* Pakistan (Kingston) 1957–58
Most Hundreds in Successive Innings
5   E. de C. Weekes (West Indies) .... 1947–48 and 1948–49
Most Hundreds in Tests
29   D. G. Bradman (Australia): 19 *v.* E, 4 *v.* SA, 2 *v.* WI, 4 *v.* I
Most Innings of Fifty and Over
63   M. C. Cowdrey (England)
Most Runs in a Series
974 (Avge 139·14)   D. G. Bradman: Australia *v.* England 1930
Most Runs in Tests
7,961 (Avge 60·77)   G. St. A. Sobers (West Indies and Rest of
the World) in 86 Tests
Highest Career Average

	Tests	Inns	NO	Runs	HS	Avge	100s	50s
D. G. Bradman (Australia)	52	80	10	6,996	334	99·94	29	13

Most Runs in a Day
309   D. G. Bradman (334): Australia *v.* England (Leeds) 1930
Most Runs Off One Over
6-ball: 22   M. W. Tate (16626) and W. Voce (1) off A. E. Hall,
E *v.* SA (Johannesburg) 1930–31
8-ball: 25   B. Sutcliffe (66061) and R. W. Blair (600) off H. J.
Tayfield, NZ *v.* SA (Johannesburg) 1953–54
Most Boundaries in an Innings
57   (5 sixes, 52 fours) J. H. Edrich (310*): E *v.* NZ (Leeds) 1965
Most Sixes in an Innings
10   W. R. Hammond (336*): E *v.* NZ (Auckland) 1932–33

4. Players' Records (Batting Partnerships)

Record Partnership for Each Wicket
1st   413   V. Mankad and P. Roy: I *v.* NZ (Madras) 1955–56
2nd   451   W. H. Ponsford and D. G. Bradman: A *v.* E (Oval) 1934
3rd   370   W. J. Edrich and D. C. S. Compton: E *v.* SA (Lord's) ... 1947
4th   411   P. B. H. May and M. C. Cowdrey: E *v.* WI (Birmingham) 1957
5th   405   S. G. Barnes and D. G. Bradman: A *v.* E (Sydney) 1946–47

6th   346   J. H. Fingleton and D. G. Bradman: A *v.* E (Melbourne) 1936–37
7th   347   D. St. E. Atkinson and C. C. Depeiza: WI *v.* A (Bridgetown) 1954–55
8th   246   L. E. G. Ames and G. O. Allen: E *v.* NZ (Lord's).........1931
9th   190   Asif Iqbal and Intikhab Alam: P *v.* E (Oval)..............1967
10th 130   R. E. Foster and W. Rhodes: E *v.* A (Sydney) 1903–04
Batsman Sharing In Most Hundred Partnerships
42   M. C. Cowdrey (England) in 187 innings

5. Players' Records (Bowling)
All Ten Wickets in an Innings
   J. C. Laker (10 for 53): England *v.* Australia (Manchester)...........1956
Most Wickets in a Match
   19   J. C. Laker (9 for 37 and 10 for 53): E *v.* A (Manchester) 1956
Most Wickets in a Series
   49   S. F. Barnes: England *v.* South Africa (4 Tests) 1913–14
Most Wickets in Tests
   307 (Avge 21·57)   F. S. Trueman (England) in 67 Tests
Hat-tricks (since 1946)
   P. J. Loader   England *v.* West Indies (Leeds) 1957
   L. F. Kline   Australia *v.* South Africa (Cape Town) 1957–58
   W. W. Hall   West Indies *v.* Pakistan (Lahore) 1958–59
   G. M. Griffin   South Africa *v.* England (Lord's)....................1960
   L. R. Gibbs   West Indies *v.* Australia (Adelaide) 1960–61
   E. J. Barlow   Rest of the World *v.* England (Leeds) 1970
Wicket with First Ball in Tests (Since 1946)
   R. Howorth   England *v.* South Africa (Oval) 1947
   Intikhab Alam   Pakistan *v.* Australia (Karachi) 1959–60
Most Wickets in Debut Match
   12   F. Martin (6 for 50 and 6 for 52) England *v.* Australia (Oval)...1890
Most Runs Conceded in an Innings
   298   L. O. Fleetwood-Smith (87-11–298-1): A *v.* E (Oval) 1938
Most Runs Conceded in a Match
   374   O. C. Scott (105·2-13–374-9): WI *v.* E (Kingston) 1929–30
Most Balls Bowled in an Innings
   588   S. Ramadhin (98-35–179-2): WI *v.* E (Birmingham) 1957
Most Balls Bowled in a Match
   774   S. Ramadhin (129-51–228-9): WI *v.* E (Birmingham) 1957

6. Players' Records (All-round Cricket)
Hundred Runs and Ten Wickets in a Match
   A. K. Davidson (44 and 80, 5 for 135 and 6 for 87): A *v.* WI
      (Brisbane) 1960–61

Hundred and Seven Wickets in First Innings
     J. M. Gregory (100 and 7 for 69): A *v*. E (Melbourne) 1920–21
Hundred and Five Wickets on Debut
     B. R. Taylor (105 and 5 for 86): NZ *v*. I (Calcutta) 1964–65
Two Thousand Runs and Two Hundred Wickets in Tests

	Tests	Runs	Wickets
G. St. A. Sobers (WI and R W)	86	7,961	226
R. Benaud (A)	63	2,201	248

7. Players' Records (Fielding)
Most Catches in an Innings
     5   V. Y. Richardson: Australia *v*. South Africa (Durban) 1935–36
Most Catches in a Match
     6   (Nine instances)
Most Catches in a Series
     15   J. M. Gregory: Australia *v*. England 1920–21
Most Catches in Tests
     121   M. C. Cowdrey (England) in 113 Tests

8. Players' Records (Wicket-keeping)
Most Dismissals in an Innings
     6 (all ct)   A. T. W. Grout: A *v*. SA (Johannesburg) 1957–58
     6 (all ct)   D. Lindsay: SA *v*. A (Johannesburg)..:.....................1966–67
     6 (all ct)   J. T. Murray: E *v*. I (Lord's) 1967
Most Dismissals in a Match
     9 (8 ct, 1 st)   G. R. A. Langley: A *v*. E (Lord's) 1956
Most Dismissals in a Series
     26 (23 ct, 3 st)   J. H. B. Waite: SA *v*. NZ (5 Tests) 1961–62
Most Catches in a Series
     24   D. Lindsay: SA *v*. A (5 Tests) 1966–67
Most Dismissals and Catches in Tests
     219 (173 ct, 46 st)   T. G. Evans (England) in 91 Tests
Most Stumpings in Tests
     52   W. A. Oldfield (Australia) in 54 Tests
Largest Total Without Byes
     659 for 8 d   T. G. Evans: England *v*. Australia (Sydney) 1946–47

C. MISCELLANEOUS RECORDS
Most Test Appearances
     113   M. C. Cowdrey (England)
Most Tests as Captain
     41   P. B. H. May (England)

Youngest Test Player
    15 years 124 days   Mushtaq Mohammad: P *v.* WI (Lahore).........1958–59
Oldest Test Player
    52 years 165 days   W. Rhodes: E *v.* WI (Kingston)..................1929–30
Most Tests as Umpire
    48   F. Chester (officiated in England between 1924 and 1955)

Index